Extraordinary Anywhere

EDITORS
INGRID HORROCKS & CHERIE LACEY

Extraordinary Anywhere
Essays on Place from Aotearoa New Zealand

VUP

TE WHARE WĀNANGA O TE ŪPOKO O TE IKA A MĀUI

VICTORIA UNIVERSITY PRESS
Victoria University of Wellington
PO Box 600 Wellington
vup.victoria.ac.nz

National Library of New Zealand
Cataloguing-in-Publication Data

Extraordinary anywhere : essays on place from Aotearoa
New Zealand / edited by Ingrid Horrocks and Cherie Lacey.
ISBN 978-1-77656-070-7
1. New Zealand essays—21st century.
I. Horrocks, Ingrid. 2. Lacey, Cherie.
NZ824.3008—dc 23

Cover and internal design by Jo Bailey and Anna Brown

Printed by Printlink in Wellington, New Zealand

Contents

You take place with you as you go on

The meshing of thought and world

Speculative Geographies

Design Colophon

Writing Here

Ingrid Horrocks
and Cherie Lacey

What's your story? It's all in the telling. Stories are compasses and architecture; we navigate by them, we build our sanctuaries and our prisons out of them, and to be without a story is to be lost in the vastness of a world that spreads out in all directions like arctic tundra or sea ice... Which means that place is a story, and stories are geography...
—Rebecca Solnit, *The Faraway Nearby*

I

Extraordinary Anywhere was first imagined on a July road trip between places. We took a break at a Paekakariki café, the breathing sea a presence just out of sight over the rise. We had only recently met and had just swapped writing for the first time.

What we realised, sitting in the warmth of that particular café in that particular place, was that despite very different styles we were in a sense trying to write the same essay. Both of us were writing, in part, about moving back to New Zealand. Ingrid's essay traversed the central North Island plateau, manoeuvring down the island to find its way back to one of the places where she grew up, a farm in the Wairarapa. Cherie was writing about the beaches west of Auckland, Pīhā, French Bay and Te Henga—not places she had inhabited so much as ones that occupied her imagination when she was living in Australia. In different ways, these places called out to us and invited us to try to put words around our feelings for them; we had both reached to the essay form for what it seemed to offer—space for contradiction and exploration, and room for both yearning and critical thought. What we also realised was that we weren't really trying to figure out what it meant to be a New Zealander, and nor were we particularly interested in the abstract idea of the nation.

We were, rather, moved by what it felt like to live in particular places here in this country, and in the intensity of feeling so many of us have about our various homes. We were struck by how many other people were also writing, talking and thinking about the distinctiveness of particular places rather than the nation-state—from creative writers and journalists, to historians and cultural theorists. Alongside this, there has been a general upsurge in essay writing in recent years—and personal essay writing especially. The first-hand accounts that we can read on blogs and in fact all over the internet are perhaps partly responsible for the steep rise in interest in personal narrative. Recent essays seemed, to us, to be taking different forms from those written by the likes of Bill Pearson, Bruce Jesson or Sandra Coney in earlier decades, which tended to address themselves directly towards the public domains of politics and economics. The change involved a shift in voice and tone, and a foregrounding of the personal without necessarily relinquishing the desire to speak of, and to, the collective or public. We became curious about what these developments signalled about our current cultural moment, and wondered what would happen if we brought some of these emerging conversations together.

The essays we solicited and have gathered in *Extraordinary Anywhere* showcase a group of New Zealand writers and thinkers not especially focused on New Zealand as such. They are interested, instead, in the obsession, fascination, wonder and often intense unease experienced in relation to particular spots in this country. They are interested in how lives are actually lived in very specific places, and how these lives—and places—have changed over time. This is, perhaps surprisingly, coupled with an interest in the wider globe to which these individual places and lives are connected—tendrils reaching out from one place to another, from one town here to an immigrant home city elsewhere, or to a location of a new diaspora. In these essays, the relationship between the local and global emerges as a fulcrum for understanding life in 21st-century Aotearoa New Zealand, superseding the imaginary, and potentially exclusionary, idea of 'the nation' or brand New Zealand.

One advantage of place-thinking is that it gets away from New Zealand as defined predominantly by its natural landscapes and environment. Most of us now live and work in cities and towns, and these are the places in which many of our most formative experiences occur. Landscape does not necessarily offer the key to our identities; nor is the landscape always the most useful background against which to think about what it means to live here. The commodifiable beauty of these islands, so readily packaged and exported, has sometimes acted as a screen, obscuring other possible understandings and narratives. Place-thinking opens up space for talking about our relationships with other kinds of locations—urban, bureaucratic, corporate, suburban, rural, and about the routes in between.

This in turn allows history to be reimagined, or rather goes hand in hand with a re-imagining of history that is already happening. A focus on particular locations moves us beyond New Zealand history as that very familiar narrative: a forward march towards national identity, with the Crown at the centre, along with the Treaty signing and two world wars. It invites closer attention to the layering of histories, including unofficial or excluded histories, personal remembrance and community stories, as well as to the physical changes to specific environments, both natural and built. Over the past few decades, regions within New Zealand have become only increasingly divergent from one another, with Auckland, for instance, as a booming immigrant city needing separate narratives of its own, and stories upon stories within those. Rural Southland is distinct from the Waikato, as it is from Hawke's Bay or Wellington, making it impossible to present any one place as a microcosm of the wider nation. Place-thinking also makes way for meditations on how unevenly settler-colonialism has been experienced by different people in different places. *Extraordinary Anywhere* heeds the calls of historian Tony Ballantyne and others for the importance of specific sites and community and global connections in understanding history. Even more important, many of the stories invoked in this collection try to express how history connects with and shapes our everyday experiences. They present models for deep understandings of history working on us, and imagine ways we could use our experiences in place to think differently about our shared futures.

New Zealanders, or at least Pākehā New Zealanders, are not famous for their eloquence, particularly when trying to speak of their feelings about living here. For Pākehā, this has sometimes led to a too-easy equation between loving the natural environment and a simplistic sense of belonging. This can end up effectively dodging more challenging understandings of how we can, and still do, occupy this place. This hesitation to speak in other ways, to narrate our experience outside this simple formula, however, could perhaps also signal a consciousness of what it means to live on settler-colonial islands in the South Pacific, where the right to speak about, or even for, Aotearoa New Zealand is a potentially fraught arena. For many Pākehā, settlers and newer migrants, the strength of emotion connected to New Zealand, to a sense of a home here, doesn't find easy expression. Many of us are aware that not being tangata whenua means that we don't have a natural, or prior, claim on this place, and so there can be an obstacle between emotion and language—we find ourselves coming up short, at times inarticulate. It can be hard to say what New Zealand means to us, to make certain claims about place, without inadvertently displacing Māori, and so, quite often, place has been a topic to be skirted around. But nor should we assume that a Māori connection to a papakāinga or 'homeplace' is clear or easily expressed, even as we acknowledge an often violent, enforced break in actual Māori inhabitation of particular locations.

Voice, then, as well as an awareness of the position from which one speaks or writes, becomes central. The personal essay offers the potential for expression that remains provisional, unsettled, challenged even, but which still conveys a strength of feeling for the places where we live and work, and which we sometimes leave behind. The authors in *Extraordinary Anywhere* write *on* place and *on* the personal essay form, and experiment with ways of writing with a kind of openness—both in the sense of opening up personal experience and in the sense of thoughts still in formation and reaching for that which might only ever be partially understood or expressed. There is a bravery in many of these pieces. They are essays in the most well-known and perhaps truest sense of the word 'essai', meaning a trial or an attempt. Our hope is that *Extraordinary Anywhere* gives a glimpse of the places we are now and how that feels, and that it will open up the range and kinds of stories we can conceive of telling about living here.

II

The collection is divided into three parts. In the first, *Any place might be extraordinary if only we knew it,* each piece focuses on a single location: Te Kūiti, Christchurch, Napier, Caversham, Brancepeth Station in the Wairarapa, and Pukeahu in central Wellington. Here place is approached as physical site, given meaning by and creating meaning from the personal and shared attachments people have to it. Poet and blogger Ashleigh Young's Te Kūiti is overlaid with music and pop stars from other places and times, transforming an 'ordinary place' into something far more resonant, potent with all the romantic longings of a teenage crush. Earthquakes can alter places beyond recognition, as explored by Sally Blundell and Cherie Lacey, where social, emotional and geographical maps are shifted in ways that make places strange, even to their long-time residents. The Christchurch earthquakes reverberate through a number of essays in the collection as a whole, both literally and as a metaphor for how place can be made and unmade, produced and erased—by geological force, by its inhabitants and by central government. Tony Ballantyne and Lydia Wevers think about archives in particular locations, and about locations themselves as archives. Their essays show what can be discovered when we pay attention to what Wevers calls, in her essay on the history of the Brancepeth farm library, the 'languages of place—paper, buildings, objects, landscape'. Ingrid Horrocks explores how Pukeahu has and could be re-imagined, through conversations, public art works, the new Pukeahu National War Memorial Park that opened on Anzac Day 2015, and a digital anthology of writing and images.

These essays respond to a more general interest, both in this country and globally, in immersions in particular places, calling to mind experiments in the essay form such as Fiona Farrell's *The Villa at the Edge of the Empire: One Hundred Ways to Read a City* (2015), about Christchurch; Joan Didion's *Where I Was From* (2003), about California; Iain Sinclair's many wandering engagements in books such as *London Orbital: A Walk Around the M25* (2002); Valeria Luiselli's mapping of urban cavities and empty spaces in *Sidewalks* (2013); and Rebecca Solnit and Rebecca Snedeker's cartographically inspired *Unfathomable City: A New Orleans Atlas* (2013). What the essays in the collection share with works such as these is a move beyond place as part of a national project, neither making it about picturesque landscapes nor about a desire to belong or to have a place to stand. Nor, we hope, do they privilege the experiences of those who live in a place to the exclusion of those newly arrived, in transit, or outside.

Some recent writing about place has felt nostalgic for the mythical idea of particular places uncontaminated by human occupation or technological development and outside influences. These hypothetical places can also be fetishised by the long-term inhabitant, who might claim a kind of authentic experience, or by the traveller, who laments the loss of an untouched landscape. However, in these essays places are formed through a layering of personal narrative and local histories, constantly and inevitably connecting with other places, here and elsewhere. Sites appear as porous and open, as contact zones where, for example, fourteen-year-old resident of Te Kūiti Ashleigh Young has an exchange with American musician Beck about the Funky Chicken, or Lydia Weavers can encounter the traces of dirt and blood left by readers more than 100 years ago. In these essays, place is always in the process of being made and re-made by what human geographer Doreen Massey calls a 'constellation of social relations, meeting and weaving together at a particular locus', such as in the casual comings and goings over decades in Ballantyne's local Caversham takeaway, run by a Chinese New Zealand family.

The essays in the second section, *You take place with you as you go on*, tell stories of mobility—of multiple places, elsewheres, non-places, dis-placements and losses of place. Here, place shows itself through personal narratives of movements between locations, both physical and mental, in which places are always constructed in relation to other places—geographic, temporal and textual. In writing about Māori connections to place, Alice Te Punga Somerville and Tina Makereti both emphasise that Māori are mobile and that 'Māori writing and Māori writing about place extend beyond places that are understood as Māori'. Te Punga Somerville ends with a migratory image of the underground streams along which eels travel, leading always to the ocean and to other shores. This in no way signals a Māori relinquishing of place. Te Punga Somerville in particular highlights the political acts involved in place-making, arguing, for example, that a place is 'produced' by us every time we name it. In relation to Wellington, she writes: 'Every time we call its name we re-place, dis-place or perhaps inadvertently mis-place Te Whanganui-a-Tara.' She also traces the personal essay back to the 19th century, to the first Māori text written in English when the author visited London, revealing a long history of Māori personal nonfiction writing.

Annabel Cooper, Alex Calder and Jack Ross also respond to New Zealand writers and their relationships to place and movement, alluding to Samuel Butler, Mary Lee, James Cowan, Keith Sinclair, Peter Wells, Dan Davin and some of the writers of the cultural nationalist period. Cooper reiterates the very practical observation of the painfully nomadic Lee that some places prove to be better than others—something that is no less true today than in Lee's 19th-century Southland. The presence of food, clean water, friends, employment opportunities and housing, as well as the security to make decisions about whether one stays or leaves, make us value some places partly by virtue of comparison. Calder and Ross show that sometimes what is most unsettling about places can only be approached through such modes as melodrama and transgressions into the supernatural. Harry Ricketts and Tina Makereti use the essay form as a vehicle of discovery for writing about their experiences—as a new migrant on the one hand, and as urban Māori with relationships to multiple homeplaces on the other. It is worth acknowledging here that many migrant and settler experiences, both historical and more recent, are not represented within the collection, something that we hope will be addressed in future gatherings of writers and nonfiction writing. Newer writers such as Tze Ming Mok and Kerry Ann Lee, as well as more established ones like Selina Tusitala Marsh, come to mind as voices that could well enrich the collective experiment begun in *Extraordinary Anywhere*.

Generally speaking, some engagements with place have seen mobility as threatening, diluting the distinctiveness of particular places. This fear involves not only goods, capital, media and people arriving, but also people leaving to go elsewhere. Perceived threats to the bounded identity of places can lead to reactionary or defensive nationalisms, like those we see at times in debates about the flag or foreign ownership of land, or more broadly in response to the newly urgent claims of refugees. The essays in this section, however, tend to imagine place through routes as well as roots, allowing for new conceptions of place that are responsive to the increasing mobility of 21st-century experiences. This is not to limit engagements with place, or to celebrate in 'absolute terms' mobility over immobility or over a sense of home, something anthropologist Ghassan Hage cautions against, suggesting that 'motion and rest, travel and homeliness' are not oppositions but 'deeply interrelated'. It is, rather, to acknowledge the potential liberation or pain of mobility and living in a mobile society, as well as the potential pleasures or claustrophobia of locatedness.

In the third section of this book, *The meshing of thought and world*, Ian Wedde, Giovanni Tiso and Tim Corballis experiment with writing about virtual and global locations, tackling subjects such as Peter Jackson, Google+ and the universe. Wedde navigates between 'orders of reality', using a piece of wood from the party tree in Middle Earth and his five-year-old granddaughter's acceptance of the 'real worlds' within movies to explore how we inhabit and are inhabited by the words and imaginings of others. Tiso reflects on his troubling experience of Google+ impersonally telling his 'story' through a set of 24 photographs taken on a trip to Camogli and Genoa. Tiso's experience with Google+ is evocative of the ways in which our experiences of place are radically altered by technologies such as mobile devices, GPS tracking systems and geotagging. As some recent textual and multimedia engagements with place have shown, digital or virtual places can have complex and enriching relationships with physical places. This is evident, for example, in projects such as Rem Koolhaas's interactive documentary *Lagos Wide and Close*, the popular app 'Drift', and in the digital Māori Maps project led by Paul Tapsell, which describes itself in its English version as a 'digital gateway' or 'portal to the marae of Aotearoa'. In the final essay, Tim Corballis seeks to negotiate how we might live with the complexity of new places, suggesting that we need to hold on to at least two perspectives: a local, individual view, which can look closely and subjectively and see the small things; but also a larger perspective, one that might include an image of the whole Earth, for example, and an imagining of place adequate to confront climate change. His essay traverses an image of the galaxy, Tuki's map, digital imagery of the ocean floor and the political possibilities of the agora. Gesturing towards the collective and what it offers, Corballis asks what kind of place we think the world could be.

III

The contributions to *Extraordinary Anywhere* take many forms, from nonfiction short stories to personal histories to pieces of embodied research. However, they are all in some way a reflection on sites and situatedness—both within the essay itself and in relation to place or places. The importance of the very particular places from which each of us speaks and views the world was highlighted when the various historians, scholars, bloggers, theorists and creative writers who appear in *Extraordinary Anywhere* gathered in Wellington in late 2014 to discuss their writing practices and how they had so far gone about telling stories of place. The real challenges of that meeting of voices, and the provocation of this essay collection which now follows, have encouraged many of the authors to mutate their writing practice, either more towards the personal or more towards the conceptual, depending on their background. The result is a series of experiments in synthesis, tentatively suggesting a number of new ways in which we might begin to write and think about the places we inhabit. If, as ecologist Geoff Park said, we need to keep 'walking and talking' our places in order to work out how to live and work in them, then innovative—and moving—new writings such as these suggest some of the very many ways this activity might be reimagined.

A sense of questioning has particular weight in Makereti's piece. For her, the essay is inevitably 'a constant argument about place', involving a circling around the 'unknowable', and inviting us 'to achieve the unattainable, like being multiple things and coming from multiple places all at once'. Makereti is not alone in her attempts. An effort to evoke the feeling of inhabiting various, and sometimes contradictory, experiences of place drives many of the essays in *Extraordinary Anywhere*. This is reminiscent of what Michel de Montaigne, the progenitor of the essay form, wrote in the 16th century: 'If my mind could gain a firm footing, I would not make essays, I would make decisions; but it is always in apprenticeship and on trial'. However, this is not to say that writing in essay form means we are not answerable to facts or politics, an issue that comes up in a number of the contributions. Nonetheless, the complexity of our embodied experiences of place finds a good fit with the questioning mode of the essay.

The rich potential of the 'narrative unreliability' (in Wedde's words) of the personal essay is what distinguishes its kind of epistemology from that of the academic essay. Our invitation to some scholars to write in a more personal form has led to these kinds of distinctions becoming a thread that runs through the collection. Ballantyne tells us something new about how the thinking of a historian can intersect with place when he describes himself leaning against the old *Indiana Jones* pinball machines in Fairways takeaways, and how, in a key academic essay of his, he drew on both Doreen Massey '(whom I openly acknowledged) and the thoughts that occurred to me in Fairways (which I didn't mention)'. Wevers describes a similar kind of 'subjective knowing' in her encounters with Brancepeth library, which she felt compelled to build into her history, 'to keep myself, as it were, in place'. Annabel Cooper, too, shows place at work on the historian, suggesting that we need both 'the kinds of evidence that the social sciences deal in' and something 'more particular and personal' to grasp the elusiveness of place in a more affective way. Lacey and Lynn Jenner contribute narratives of their own relinquishment of psychoanalytic and psychological world views in exchange for the complex self-positioning of first person writing.

Other contributors explicitly reflect on and perform ways in which ideas can emerge from places. Horrocks, Jenner and Wedde all write about how ideas evolve in the construction of an essay. Horrocks narrates how her understanding of Pukeahu developed through visits to the campus marae, discussions with those with claims to the place, and a series of walks. Walking also plays a role in Wedde's methodology, giving us an insight into the mind of a writer alert to possibilities for new writing, and Jenner presents both an essay and a commentary on how the ideas for her piece developed over a period of months. In all three there is the presence of ongoing conversations, notebooks filling up with, as Wedde writes, the 'little shock of *noticing*', and explorations of how these notes get shaped in writing.

Some of the essays more implicitly demonstrate the extent to which the intensely personal can be used for explorations that extend far beyond the self. Young and Lacey use the form to evoke the tenderness and tension of relationships between local history enthusiast fathers and their mobile daughters, invoking a dynamic, if often unspoken, intergenerational dialogue about place. Ricketts and Ross evoke friendships, showing how the place of our minds is inhabited by intimates who live—and die—elsewhere. In Blundell's piece on Christchurch, the personal *is* collective, figured through the 'we' of the first person plural, which in her essay denotes the many voices of the people of Christchurch who hope, 'in the cracks in the planning', to shape the 'shared space' of their future city.

These essays evoke what Jenner calls, quoting one person quoting another about another, 'the metaphysical feeling of the strangeness of existence'. All are characterised by openness and are animated by a search, allowing for a subjective investment and even, at times, a vulnerability. Makereti writes of her own writing practice, 'there is a tension from the first line—this is how I know I should keep writing. Even now I feel it, the impossibility of making what I'm trying to say clear, transparent, sensible, straightforward even'. It is this sense of tension, of trial and attempt—detectable in all of the essays here in various ways—that we hope will keep people reading *Extraordinary Anywhere*.

Wellington, February 2016

Notes on Sources:

References in this introduction come from Doreen Massey, 'A Global Sense of Place', *Space, Place, and Gender* (Cambridge: Polity Press, 1994), 154; Ghassan Hage, 'In conversation with Dimitri Papadopoulos: Migration, Hope and the Making of Subjectivity in Transnational Capital', *International Journal for Critical Psychology* 12 (2004), 115; Māori Maps: http://www.maorimaps.com/; Rem Koolhas, *Lagos Wide and Close*: http://lagos.submarinechannel.com/; Michel de Montaigne, 'Of Repentance', *The Complete Essays of Montaigne*, trans Donald M. Frame (Stanford: Stanford University Press, 1957), 611; and Geoff Park, 'Looking for Signs of Life — Nature and the Genius Loci in the Austral City' (1997), *Theatre Country: Essays on Landscape and Whenua* (Wellington: Victoria University Press, 2006), 45.

Recent writing and thinking about place in New Zealand includes Tony Ballantyne's ongoing historical work, discussed in his essay in this collection; Steve Braunias, *Civilisation: Twenty Places on the Edge of the World* (Wellington: Awa Press, 2012); Alex Calder, *The Settler's Plot: How Stories Take Place in New Zealand* (Auckland: Auckland University Press, 2011); Martin Edmond's nonfiction writings over two decades, most recently *The Dreaming Land* (Wellington: Bridget Williams Books, 2015); the developing work of Gregory O'Brien on the ways in which paintings and poems can speak to, for and of, a place, including the ongoing Kermadec art project; Joan Metge, *Tuamaka: The Challenge of Difference in Aotearoa New Zealand* (Auckland: Auckland University Press, 2010); Janet Stephenson, Mick Abbott and Jacinta Ruru (eds.), *Beyond the Scene: Landscape and Identity in Aotearoa New Zealand* (Dunedin: Otago University Press, 2010); Alice Te Punga Somerville's *Once Were Pacific: Māori Connections to Oceania* (Minneapolis: University of Minnesota Press, 2012), which considers indigenous writing in relation to diaspora and migrations rather than to the bounded place of the nation state; and Stephen Turner, 'Settler Dreaming', *Memory Connection* 1.1 (2011): 115–26.

There has also been a general upsurge in the publishing of (creative) nonfiction writing in recent years, some of which involves engagements with particular locations, as in the 'My Auckland' issue of *Landfall* (2012), or in Anna Sanderson's 'A Red Brick Church' in her collection *Brainpark* (Wellington: Victoria University Press, 2006); or, with changing New Zealand identity more generally, as exemplified in Julianne Schultz and Lloyd Jones's introduction to the *Pacific Highways* issue of *Griffith Review* (2013). More widely, there is the Bridget Williams Books Texts series of long essays launched in 2014; and *Tell You What: Great New Zealand Nonfiction*, the annual also started in 2014, which draws extensively on blog publications, itself one of the foremost modes for the creation and dissemination of personal forms of nonfiction writing.

Acknowledgements

We are grateful to all those who have supported this project over the past year and a half. Thank you to the W.H. Oliver Humanities Research Academy at Massey University, the Stout Research Centre for New Zealand Studies at Victoria University and the Centre for Research on Colonial Culture at the University of Otago, who jointly supported the 'Placing the Personal Essay Colloquium' which we convened on Massey's Wellington campus in December 2014. This event brought all the writers involved together in a single place for a vital period of conversation.

We would also like to acknowledge the authors themselves. Participation in the project was by invitation and every single person we asked accepted our invitation and has stuck with us. Thank you for engaging with the provocation of the project so willingly, for putting up with our suggestions that you do a little more of this or that and for being so enthusiastic about the project throughout. You were a pleasure to work with.

For their design we are immensely grateful to Jo Bailey and Anna Brown, who came into the project as design researchers early on and had an impact not just on how the book looks, but on how the text has been arranged and shaped. We would also like to thank the College of Creative Arts at Massey University for their contribution towards the collaborative design research undertaken.

At Victoria University Press, we would like to thank Ashleigh Young and Fergus Barrowman for their creative input and astute guidance throughout the project, as well as to Holly Hunter, for her role in meticulously copyediting the text. Anna Sanderson also provided us with a wonderfully helpful peer review.

On a more personal level, we would like to thank our families: Tim, Natasha and Lena, and John and Emilia (who was born between the colloquium and book). Cherie would especially like to thank her mother-in-law Joanne for her care of Emilia, which enabled Cherie's ongoing participation in this work.

Any place might be extraordinary if only we knew it

The Te Kūiti Underground

Ashleigh Young

It seems to me that the realest reality lives somewhere beyond the edge of human vision.

—*Russell Hoban*

Halfway up View Road, I turned to look back the way I had come. View Road was a gravel road, a dead end. Below me was a crosshatching of paddocks and roads and the sewage pond, and you could see Te Kūiti Airport. This wasn't really an airport at all but a well-groomed field with poplar trees at each end and a tumbledown house, the club house, where the pilots, including my father, gathered. It was just another paddock, the planes large animals.

As I stood looking, catching my breath, a young man appeared around the corner about 100 metres away. I felt a small leap in my chest. He'd been following me, I thought. Looking for me. He'd had a hunch I would be out walking, and now here he was. I heard the crunch of his boots on the gravel as he approached. Perhaps I should have turned and walked away, avoiding his eyes, but I stayed very still. The man was wearing a grey T-shirt, the collarless sort with a few buttons below the neck. Straight-legged blue jeans. He was also wearing sandals, which was a bit unusual. As he got closer he raised his eyebrows and made a slight pout, and, I swear, his head wobbled a bit from side to side. He reached for my hand. Yes. It was Paul McCartney.

Specifically, it was Paul McCartney as he appeared in his picture in the sleeve notes of *The White Album*: unshaven, almost dishevelled looking. His fringe was just riffling his eyebrows; his eyes were a sad liquid. Together we began to walk, hand in hand. I noted that Paul McCartney's fingers were slightly calloused. Of course: he'd just finished playing the bass on the greatest album of all time. We walked slowly to the top of View Road, then we looked out at the hills, trees, roads, cows, the interlocking parts of nowhere. We talked about music, books, writing, our families. I had a lot to say to Paul but much of it wasn't ready to form words, so it filled my chest like a balloon. Still, Paul looked at me sideways, nodding in agreement as I didn't talk.

It was 1997. The Beatles had split nearly 30 years before. Paul McCartney's face was beginning its slow collapse. Anyone coming the other way on View Road—not that there was ever anyone—would have seen a grim-faced girl with her hand flapping out at one side as she walked.

As my favourite bands changed, Paul became mutable. He would start out as Paul and on the way home become George. A few times he was Tom Petty, wearing a black hat, then Billy Corgan before he lost his hair. For a good long while he was Thom Yorke, his lazy eye fluttering in the harsh light. And soon he was Beck too, loping along in sneakers and acid-washed jeans, occasionally shrieking with laughter like he did on *Stereopathic Soul Manure*. It was enough to imagine a warm, intelligent presence, but this presence was always a musician from a stage or studio in a big city from somewhere in the world. It was always someone who could make an ordinary place, an ordinary moment, more intense, more like a film, something driven towards meaningful conclusion.

I'd told myself stories before and sometimes written them down, before sending them off to the editor of the *New Zealand School Journal*, whose address I'd copied from the inside cover of a Part 3 journal at school. There was a hedgehog that went hang-gliding off the top of Mangarino Road. There was an intricate messaging system among the tiny crayfish in the streams in the bush above our house. Aliens had crash-landed their UFO in the bush and now had a secret colony there! My stories received polite rejection letters from the editor at the *School Journal*, which I showed to my parents with sorrow. But I was fourteen now, and I wanted to be part of the story. I wanted to walk beside someone from a different universe who would make Te Kūiti into something else. Its army-blanket green would become a romantic backdrop, the same way the desert was a romantic backdrop in *The English Patient*, instead of just lonely and hostile.

At the same time, the landscape of Te Kūiti sometimes created a delicious sadness in me. The hills, the row of pines above a clay bank, the Te Kūiti sky, a smothering grey—these surroundings confirmed and enhanced my loneliness. I didn't have many friends at high school, I didn't have a boyfriend, and although I wanted to be a writer, I wanted more to be in a band and be very famous. I had a limited sense of the ridiculous but a strong sense of the melodramatic, and I gathered the landscape into my mood as if gathering up a luxurious fabric, pulling it round me and breathing it in. I believed that no one living in Te Kūiti had ever felt the same as I felt.

One day I wrote a fan letter to Beck, whose album *Odelay* had just come out at the CD store on Rora Street. 'Dear Beck, I have never written a fan letter before'—this, of course, was a blatant lie; I had written to many famous people, including Paul McCartney—'but I wanted to write to say how much I love *Odelay*.' I imagined Beck reading the letter, slightly distracted at first and then drawn in by my words, marvelling that his music had travelled all the way to the bottom of the world to a girl who lived in a town he would never have known existed, if not for my letter.

A few weeks, perhaps a month later, I received a reply from Beck. Or from someone pretending to be him. The letter said: 'Wow, what's it like living in New Zealand? Do y'all have the Funky Chicken there?—Beck.' I read the letter over and over, my hands shaking, until it ceased to make sense. Although, I had to admit, the letter hadn't made much sense from the start. What was the Funky Chicken? Was it a dance, a food, a fast food joint? What amazed me was not just that Beck had written back to me. It was that he had written the words 'New Zealand'. He'd said the secret code word that granted us access to the rest of the world. And he was interested to know what it was like here. It didn't seem an idle interest but a genuine one. He was so interested that he'd said 'Wow'.

Of course, I wrote a long letter in reply. No, as far as I knew we didn't have the Funky Chicken: what was it exactly? I told him about my town, how its closest city was Hamilton, and that every year we had a celebration called Midnight Madness, when all the shops stayed open till midnight, and there was a sheep-shearing competition at the Civic Centre. Te Kūiti men were so fast at shearing, I told Beck, that the town was known as the Shearing Capital of the World. I wrote about this mockingly, as if talking about a classmate who I'd decided was a moron. I told him about how the Mangaokewa River often flooded and made the riverbank muddy so I couldn't walk my dog there. I also told him in some detail about walking up View Road and imagining him walking with me, in his checked shirt and jeans and old sneakers, the same outfit he'd worn in that interview in *Spin Magazine*.

I didn't hear from Beck again. But the first letter made me feel that I was destined for great things.

As I played the piano and howled into the lounge, singing about the broken heart I hadn't yet experienced, I sometimes thought about being on a stage with my brother JP. It was JP who was becoming famous. He was doing a songwriting course in Hamilton and he had a four-track recording machine. He'd had a song on student radio and he regularly played gigs with his band The Clampers, who had a small but devoted following. To my father, this pursuit of music was baffling. Nobody made any money writing songs, certainly nobody who came from a town of farmers, electricians and accountants like him. 'You've got to have money coming in,' he told my brother. 'You can't not have money coming in.' In secret, JP and I would make fun of his belligerent voice. *Gotta have money coming in. Gotta have money coming in.* It became a kind of chant.

Despite this, I knew that Dad liked to hear JP play. He would cajole him into playing at his friends' milestone birthday parties. (Sometimes JP would impersonate Dad: '*Play some Eagles, JP. They'll love it. Play Hotel California!* I feel like a performing monkey.') When JP relented and got out his guitar, Dad looked as happy as I had ever seen him. Leaning on the bar, awkward with pride.

And we had all been proud, though in my case envious too, when JP had auditioned to play at 'Neil Finn and Friends' in Hamilton and had been chosen to play alongside the man himself—Neil Finn, the great Neil Finn. There was a photo in the *Waikato Times* of the two of them standing on the stage, looking uncannily like brothers: blond hair, long arms, guitars held at the same angle. JP is mid-song, wide-eyed in the expensive-looking spotlight. He looks braced, maybe hitting a high note. Neil Finn is holding out one hand towards him as if presenting JP to the world.

When JP came home to Te Kūiti on occasional weekends or at term break, Dad would corner him in the kitchen. 'I was talking to a bloke at OMYA,' he might begin. OMYA was the limeworks across the railway line from the airport. It was a place of blinding white gravel and cooling towers and mini forklift trucks constantly in reverse. 'I thought we could set up some work.' He would look at JP with a funny expression, leaving the words on the brink. *You can't not have money coming in.* We'd all stand there in the kitchen, Dad in his office clothes, me in my high school uniform, Mum in an apron with her glass of

Country cask wine, and JP in his cardigan and cord pants, plumes of blond hair sticking up around his head. He had been writing songs all day and recording them in the bathroom, for the acoustics. 'All right, I'll have a think about it,' he'd say unhappily. Many of the worst jobs he's ever had began this way.

My father had lived in Te Kūiti his whole life. So had his parents. He was born there and now his name was on a sign outside an accountancy firm. He seemed to always be on his way to and from the office in his blue Fiat Tipo, his only passengers the many lever-arch files sliding around in the back seat. Or he was off to rehearsals for the town plays that he acted in. He lived deeply inside the town, was known to everybody, and perhaps because of this, he seemed to live elsewhere from me. As I got older, we had less and less to say to each other. By the time I was ten we had stopped speaking to each other much at all. I avoided him and he seemed to avoid me too. I watched as he made people laugh on the stage, with his hair talcum-powdered grey, playing various comically unhinged old men—a vicar, a murderer, a hapless husband.

He also had a forensic knowledge of Te Kūiti, and this made him even more difficult for me to understand. Why would you bother learning about this place? There was nothing here. But he knew the town from all directions, because as well as being an accountant he was a pilot. From the back seat of his four-seater Cherokee, squashed between my mother and one of my brothers, I would watch him at the controls. And despite myself, when I studied the back of his head, the fat headphones cushioning his ears and a microphone under his chin, a profound trust rose in me. He knew where he was going and exactly how to get there, whether we were going as far as Oamaru, where my grandparents lived, or to Kinloch or Raglan, where we would swim. He knew how to fly through storms that threw us sideways, through blanketing fog and bulleting rains. He knew how to do aerobatics—loops, spins, rolls, vertical lines—though I'd only ever seen this from the ground, looking up with horror, wondering if he was shouting swearwords inside the cockpit. My trust of his knowledge felt uncomfortably like love. He knew Te Kūiti's history and geography in detail, and when we were all flying together as a family he would point things out to us: rivers, lakes, the houses and farms of people we knew.

Watching him manoeuvre a landing was impressive: there was something triumphant in it, and, especially when emerging from difficult flights, something almost maniacal in his focus. He was like Batman bearing down on a villain in his Batmobile. He'd guide the plane towards the runway, flicking switches and twiddling various knobs, and burbling into a radio. At some point he'd reach a hand up and crank the lever on the ceiling that controlled the plane's nose, the movement a bit like spinning a lasso. The familiar trees and grass stretched up to meet us, and then solid ground was rushing under our wheels. I was always grateful for his calculations and focus at the moment when he returned us to land. There was something magical in how he did it every time. I didn't tell him that, though.

The curious thing was that my father, for all his fixations on money and a sensible career path, had once played music too—had once been in a band, of sorts. He would not let us forget this. He had evidence, and his evidence was the Washhouse Tapes. The Washhouse Tapes. They insisted that they belonged to a better, more hopeful, more creative time. As long as the tapes existed, and surely they would exist forever, this time would never really go away.

'The Washhouse Tapes' was actually a single battered cassette tape. It was called the Washhouse Tapes because some years after it was made, then lost, then forgotten, it was salvaged from a washhouse. Whose washhouse? No one knew, other than that it was a derelict one. But the origins on the tape were even more uncertain. They were songs that my father and his best friend, Hutch, had made when they were teenagers, with their girlfriends—my mother Julia, and Jenny—mostly on backing vocals. Why had the songs been written? What had the band wanted to happen?

The group recorded the songs in the late 60s and early 70s in a cabin at Mōkau Beach, a West Coast fishing town about an hour's drive from Te Kūiti.

A World War II sea mine is mounted on a plinth in the centre of the township, having been washed up on the beach in 1942. At the time of recording, my dad was a young accounting student and ham radio enthusiast, and his friend Hutch was a budding singer-songwriter and rugby writer.

Hutch was the one with the good voice. I thought he sounded a bit like Brian Wilson, his voice full and pure. But my father did not have a good singing voice. It was reedy and tuneless and also held a strange urgency, which seemed to exacerbate the reediness. While Hutch sang tunefully and played guitar, banjo, piano, or accordion, Dad would just roar while bashing on a beer crate, slapping his thighs, hitting a coalscuttle with a stick, or making beeping noises on his ham radio set. In the recordings he sounds like a kid still discovering the magic of recording noises and being able to play them back to himself afterwards. He reminds me of the actor in the town shows—unleashed from himself, somehow.

The songs held echoes of their favourite music at the time, like Bob Dylan, the Beach Boys, and the Beatles. You could hear it in the harmonies, the chord changes. At the same time, the songs—which had been recorded by bouncing tracks between tape recorders so as to build up layers of sound—were of small-town New Zealand. The lyrics referenced places like Ruatoria, Mōkau, Otahuhu, Porirua, Hangatiki. But then, every so often, there would be somewhere else. 'Went on down to Santa Fe,' Hutch crooned, or 'I'm just a punk . . . at Punk Junction.' Wherever that was.

It's true that many of the songs were meant to be absurd. You could tell by looking at the titles. 'Meals on Wheels on Fire', 'Deaf Monkey', 'Waiting for My Eggs to Come', 'Amazing Grapes', 'Yodelling Night Cart Man'. In 'Let Us Pray', which ridiculed the church services they'd had to go to as kids, and which they still felt compelled to attend, Dad began repeatedly roaring at the top of his lungs, like a minister who had finally lost it at his congregation, 'LET US PRAY' until the song sputtered out. There were other songs that ended similarly—they broke up into discordant noise, as if all of the instruments had suddenly disintegrated.

A lot of the songs just broke up into discordant noise. But there were one or two songs that were quieter, almost tender, like one called 'Gartho', which Hutch's girlfriend Jenny sang, as she played piano. The song was just about missing someone named Gartho, who I thought must have moved away.

My parents would have dinner parties, and they'd get out the tape. I'd hear the familiar tinny racket, the voices crackling out, the piano with its yellow-sounding keys. I'd retreat to my room while they sat around crying with laughter. Every so often the battered cassette tape would be chewed up by the tape deck, and the creased magnetic spools would have to be teased out and rewound. Hutch and Jenny's two daughters, Jessie and Sarah, hated the precious tape even more than I did, and protested vehemently, cruelly, whenever one of our dads put it on. Jessie once shouted, finally, 'No one wants to hear your music, Dad,' while Hutch, now a man in his fifties with greying ginger hair and aviator spectacles, acquiesced and gently ejected the tape from the machine.

In the early 2000s I'd take the night train from Wellington to Te Kūiti, listening to the *White Album* on my Walkman the whole way. Once, it was just my father who came to meet me. I got off the train onto the freezing platform at three o'clock in the morning. There he was in his railway-station-meeting clothes: a hooded duffel coat, hands in pockets.

The flat where he lived now was small and chilly, with dishes in the sink, towels on the floor, no pictures on the walls, an unfamiliar view of Te Kūiti through the window—you could see across to the other side of the valley, where we had lived before. That house had been sold, because my mother had moved to the South Island for a teaching job and my father was getting ready to go too. He just needed time to wrap up his business. 'It's a major upheaval,' I heard him insist more than once, in response to why he was taking so long, 'major upheaval.'

After a few hours of sleep in a fold-out bed in his study, and before he left for work that morning, he made us coffee. I watched him carrying out a long-winded filtering method using an old hand grinder and a grease-stained plastic funnel. I recognised the funnel from our garage. I'd used it a few times to funnel milk powder into plastic bottles for newborn lambs. And Dad had funnelled oil into the car with it.

'What is this? What are you doing?'

'What's the problem?' he said. 'Gets the job done.' And he tried to show me the method he had invented, but I shook my head.

We drank the coffee silently at the kitchen table. I thought I could taste the old garage.

In my half-awake state, the filtering method made me feel melancholy, as if it was a sign of my dad and I drifting still further apart. I imagined various bits of detritus from our old lives across the town becoming strange tools in his solitary life. I imagined him becoming stranger and stranger in my eyes, and me becoming more narrow-minded in his. I thought of him alone in Te Kūiti, in purgatory.

The next day, while he was at work, I walked to the other side of town and up View Road. There was the smothering grey sky, the paddocks and gravel roads. Here was the cows' silent evaluation as I walked by. And in the distance, the airport. I thought about my boyfriend, a drummer in a band, and how thrilling it was that we'd recently held hands in the back of a car. As I dwelled on this, my excitement made me feel almost physically sick. And then it seemed to me that Te Kūiti had somehow grown even smaller.

That was the last time I visited. Soon, finally, my father would move away too, but he would still get the Te Kūiti newspaper delivered to their new address, and he would frequently visit, flying up from the south and landing at the old airfield over the poplars. He liked to race himself flying over the Cook Strait, getting his time as short as possible. He got it down to 18 minutes once.

*

Te Kūiti, 1964.
The Beatles had conquered England and the States
and they made their presence felt down in the King Country . . .

These were the opening lines of a song called 'The Te Kūiti Underground', which my brother, still defiantly playing music, wrote in 2011. The song went on to tell the story of two questing musicians, 'Garth' and 'Pete'. Inspired by the Beatles, they try to create 'the ultimate pop masterpiece' to set alight the musical and pastoral landscape of provincial New Zealand in the 1960s. They take their reel-to-reel four-track tape machine out to a bach at Mōkau Beach, where they record the songs in a creative frenzy. But, of course, the music they make is doomed to obscurity. Perhaps it is too ahead of its time, the men tell each other, and they resign themselves to ordinary lives. The story takes a tragic turn: years pass, the bach at Mōkau is swept away in a storm, and eventually both of the men die in horrible ways—Garth gets drunk one night and falls asleep on the main trunk line, while Pete dies alone and bitter after a divorce. Pete's two sons return to Te Kūiti to clean out their father's flat, and in a corner of his garden shed, they find a dusty cardboard box. Inside: the reel-to-reel four-track tape machine, and inside that, the tape.

It was when I heard this song that I thought of the Washhouse Tapes differently. There was some kind of yearning for other places and other lives in the songs. But there was also a romanticism of the King Country: it was as if this place, for my father and his friends, was as potent as Liverpool in the 1960s. Maybe it was something close to what I had felt as I walked in the Te Kūiti hills imagining Paul McCartney at my side: a need to make something more, to see something more than what there was. Perhaps I could even sense the yearning as a kid, when we played the songs on car trips to Mōkau where we spent our summers. But I wasn't yet able to recognise what it was that I was hearing.

Ashleigh Young writes poetry and nonfiction. Her collection of essays won the 2009 Adam Foundation Prize and an essay from the collection won the 2009 *Landfall* essay competition. She has published a poetry collection, *Magnificent Moon* (Victoria University Press, 2012), and her essays have appeared in *Sport*, *Tell You What*, the *Griffith Review* (Australia), *Five Dials* (UK), and on her personal blog, eyelashroaming.com. An essay collection, *Can You Tolerate This?*, is published by VUP in 2016. She teaches an undergraduate workshop in creative science writing with Dr Rebecca Priestley and works as an editor at Victoria University Press.

Reoccupying Christchurch: Dancing on the Edge of Disaster

Sally Blundell

1. It's no use going back to yesterday, because I was a different person then. —*Alice*

Oakland, California, 1935. After a 45-year absence American writer Gertrude Stein returns to her hometown in what was once pastoral California. She finds a changed city. The population is 10 times what it was when she left at the age of 17. Her family home is gone, the rural landscape of her childhood now an urban centre. As she writes two years later in *Everybody's Autobiography*, 'what was the use of my having come from Oakland it was not natural to have come from there yes write about it if I like or anything if I like but not there, there is no there there.' While some residents were affronted—was it a slight, a comment on the port city's lack of culture or intellectualism?—Stein's observation was a succinct reaction to a moment of non-recognition, a radical disconnection between the home turf of childhood memories and a burgeoning metropolis. The physical there-ness of her personal history had been eradicated, grown over, built out. No longer could she rely on the complex of remembered landmarks, buildings, sights, smells that anchor people to place, both historically and imaginatively. As Kelly Baker writes, cities are storehouses for personal and collective memory. The 'nesting' of one's life narrative within these larger, more historic stories of place 'extend not only one's connection to a particular place, but also, through collective narratives of group origin myths, in a more symbolic and imaginative way, to the fellow inhabitants of that place.'[2]

What is there to do, to be, in a hometown that bears no semblance to home? What happens when 'that place' is suddenly, dramatically, altered beyond recognition?

2. 'However,' he said, brightening up a little, 'we haven't had an earthquake lately.' — *A.A. Milne*

Christchurch, 2011. Days after the February 22 earthquake we begin our circumnavigation, tracking the wire-fenced cordon that encircles the ragged core of Christchurch's urban 'red zone'. By night it is a black absence within a dim periphery of street lights; by day, an unfathomable collapse of stone, glass and steel, rucked roads and gaping walls. For two years we hold our vigil, skirting a contracting barricade, bearing witness to a city that continues to fall long after the initial 40 seconds of tectonic upheaval. (An earlier earthquake, on 4 September 2010, was larger on the Richter scale but caused far less devastation — we had, we thought, survived 'the big one'.) The numbers: 185 people dead, 900 buildings demolished within the four avenues, 200 heritage listings lost to the arc and bend of the excavator's arm, the grip of a grapple bucket. Still we stop and stare at the gaping fractures in the place we called home, searching within the stark functionality of rescue, recovery and demolition for the serendipitous locales of personal and collective identity: the first flat, the favourite café, the place of a first kiss, first job, first fall. We are out of sync with this battered city. Our social, emotional, geographical maps have been changed, corrupted, made strange. As Banks Peninsula writer Fiona Farrell notes, 'It's easy, in this tumble of feeling and fact, to lose the way.'[3]

In *The Villa at the Edge of Empire* (2015) Farrell describes the condition of solastalgia, a word coined by Australian philosopher Glenn Albrecht to describe the chronic distress caused by unwanted changes to home and landscape, a neologism combining the melancholia of nostalgia and the eradication of home-based solace resulting from the breakdown of the relationship between home and one's 'psychic identity'. As Albrecht writes, '[Solastagia] is the "lived experience" of negative environmental change when your sense of place is under attack . . . It is the homesickness you have when you are still at home.'[4]

Confronted with the abrupt force of a natural disaster, that sense of attack is more intense, the sense of disconnection (like that described by Stein) more acute. As architectural historian Jessica Halliday says, cities normally change at a pace equivalent to the rest of life. 'From childhood to teenagehood through to going to university and early adulthood—even if you are not there the whole time, a city changes at a rate that is commensurate with your own life changes. But in Christchurch change has been sudden and disruptive—and that is psychologically difficult.'[5]

3. They are waiting on the shingle — will you come and join the dance?
— The Mock Turtle

Through ongoing aftershocks, faced with a ruptured and still frightening city, we danced. Just weeks after the first earthquake of 2010, an inner-city site made vacant by a collapsed building thrummed with music. A small audience sat on toadstool seats and fake grass as a cello duo played in a street of mangled awnings. The two-week event, organised by newly formed urban regeneration programme Gap Filler, was unexpected, incongruous in its surroundings, but there we sat on borrowed stools facing catastrophe with a song and a beer in hand.

Following the February 22 earthquake Gap Filler took once more to what was now a glut of sites left empty by fallen or demolished buildings. Week after week, month after month, a Facebook calendar of grassroots events drew us back to the appalling bleakness of a city in ruins. A book exchange in a double-doored commercial fridge, a painted Monopoly-board property, a pétanque court, a mini-golf course, a cycle-powered cinema, a bowling alley, a community pizza oven. In the face of physical and emotional trauma and massive social disruption, it was a defiantly playful response to an inconceivable urban environment.

'We were trying to create ways for people to come back to the central city,' says Gap Filler co-founder Ryan Reynolds. 'To generate interest, so people would care what happens.'[6] This was not spectacle. We had done with stultifying spectacle. Rather, it was an invitation to participate, to plan, to play, to talk, to insist on admittedly small assertions of control in a city battered by uncontrollable forces.

Throughout Gap Filler's history, says Reynolds, those assertions have been open, inclusive, exploratory.

'We look at site, we look at the social context of the city, the political context, the physical context, what is needed, what is missing, what could start a good discussion. So it is propositional. It is testing a hypothesis. It is providing a framework for participation. We have explored loads of different ways of doing that but that is at the core of every one of our projects.'

In 2012 designers, businesses and volunteers pitched in to construct the Pallet Pavilion, a temporary arena made from 3000 borrowed blue pallets on a central corner site left vacant by the demolition of the Crowne Plaza Hotel. Within the large, Lego-like soundshell, on the edge of what was Christchurch's historic market square, we met for coffee, performances, pop-up feasts and market days. It was messy, provisional. Prime inner-city real estate reconfigured into a flexible, temporary space for public art and experimentation.

That year too the Dance-o-Mat, comprising a timber floor, a string of lights and a set of speakers linked to a coin-operated washing machine with an iPod connection, became an open invitation for people to dance within a landscape of shattered buildings, on the literal edge of disaster. As Gap Filler co-founder Coralie Win explains, some warned it wouldn't work: 'They said

Christchurch people wouldn't dance in public.'[7] But we did. We do. Flamenco dancers, hip hop crews, a swing dance troupe, parents, children, the Superhero Dance Squad — stamping and spinning and jumping and jiving on a wall-less dance floor. Despite its lack of borderedness, and its peripatetic movement around the uncertain heart of the city, it has come to define a space, a place, a provocative opportunity.

Others also took to the streets. Guerrilla gardeners lobbed clay seed bombs into fenced sites. Street artists took cans, brushes and rollers to suddenly exposed or half-collapsed walls. The newly formed Greening the Rubble urban ecology initiative established pocket parks and community gardens on vacant land. The Plant Gang fed, nurtured and replanted wild plants. Food trucks, poetry walls and street sculptures seeded and spread. Downtown businesses established the inner city Re:Start Mall made of refurbished shipping containers. In late 2012 the Christchurch City Council helped establish Life in Vacant Spaces (LiVS) to broker the temporary use of privately owned land in the city centre. It was colourful, chaotic, uneven in its notability but instrumental in bringing people back into the city. All re-activated spaces given over to weeds, rubble and, for some, terrifying memories. All maintained tenuous bridges to a city gone and a city yet to be. All worked to retain a *there* there.

This is not new. Around the world, artist collectives and community groups have been re-activating empty retail spaces and stalled developments through art projects, pop-up shops and pocket gardens in what London's guerrilla gardener Richard Reynolds describes as a widespread war 'against neglect and scarcity of public space'.[8] But this was a different war. This was a reclamation of place, public interference in what was becoming an increasingly contested process of city-making, a community-driven and supported programme of events that anchored us to an unrecognisable environment and gave us a model, a radical exemplar, of what participatory urban design could be. Maybe not everywhere, says Ryan Reynolds, 'and maybe not the only way, but there is a big opportunity to construct flexible frameworks for participation.'

4. And YOU are the one who'll decide where to go. — *Dr Seuss*

What to do with a broken city? In November 2011 the Christchurch City Council orchestrated the Share-an-Idea public forum. Over three days people used Post-it Notes, Lego, video links, formal submissions and drawings to describe what sort of city they wanted. The resulting Draft Central City Recovery Plan called for 'a more sustainable, people-scale environment, where the city's waterways and natural environment play a substantial role.'[9] It included cycleways, narrower streets, more green spaces, a wider Avon River corridor, a commuter rail system, sustainable housing, a more human-scale central city.

The government shook its head. A wish list, said Canterbury Earthquake Recovery Minister Gerry Brownlee. A new government agency was formed under the mantel of the Canterbury Earthquake Recovery Authority (CERA): the Christchurch City Development Unit, tasked with developing a new plan, a roadmap to much-needed business confidence.

In July 2012, after a heroic 100 (actually closer to 70) days, a new blueprint was presented to the country, a grand plan articulating a smaller city centre within a green frame punctuated by several large-scale anchor projects — a new convention centre, stadium, library, sports facility, bus interchange (no commuter rail) — and designated precincts: innovation here; retail there; performing arts, health, justice there, there and there.

'The blueprint went from a council document that was aspirational to something entirely object-focused,' says Ryan Reynolds. 'A lot of these objects existed in the council plan but without the rest of that constellation of incentives and coherence and principles of urban design the initial excitement was more muted.'

But the pressure was on. There was a city to build. Insurance payouts to hold to the city. Potential investors to assure. Negotiations with property owners began. Demolition orders were given. Government tenants signed up. But opposition to the plan was also growing. Questions were being asked. Do we need a new stadium, right on the edge of a city? Should a replacement convention centre, with its sporadic use, be positioned so close to the city centre? In a city with so many demands on the public purse, why should we help fund these government projects? Who made these decisions? Who asked us?

Those in charge of the rebuild were accused of ignoring residents, of ignoring, rather than utilising, the strength of their connection to the city. What has changed most in Christchurch, says Halliday, is the built form and our relationship to it. 'But we got shut out of it, first physically, then politically.'

The government created a situation by wiping out an inner city, says George Parker from Christchurch's Free Theatre and fellow graduate from the University of Canterbury's Theatre and Film Studies with Reynolds. 'By thinking of the city as a *tabula rasa* they underestimated what a city is, how a sense of place exists through memory and desire. The politicians, economists and master planners have under-appreciated the value of history, perhaps because this is a relatively young city. But it is this youth in a still transitional post-colonial culture that makes heritage and a sense of place all the more precious.'

Now the sheer scale of some of the think-big anchor projects, he says, is daunting. 'You have to find some perspective that is not just about monster buildings and monster precincts but that is more orientated to people's perceptions at street level. Less a god's-eye view from above and more a bottom-up view from the cracks in the pavement.'[10]

He points to the new home for the Free Theatre, recently re-opened in the former gymnasium of the old Canterbury College, now the Arts Centre.

'We don't need a big Barbican-style place to put all the arts, but a centre that is young and dynamic, responsive to change, trying out new ways to bring people together.'

Despite assurances of imminent activity, new developments have been slow to begin. The green frame has been reduced in scale and ambition. The winning design for a new inner-city residential venture, another of the anchor projects, has foundered. As of early 2016, the $284 million convention centre development, spanning two prime inner-city blocks, remains snagged on uncertainty and rumours of developer retreat. Talk of the new stadium has gone quiet. Treasury has raised concerns about the viability of some of the anchor projects.

In the meantime, private sector investment is gathering momentum. Key tenants — banks, government departments, hotels, chain retail outlets — are adding their logos to artists' visualisations of planned developments. Already many of the skeletal forms of new inner-city developments promise a monumentalism at odds with Christchurch's small, owner-occupier commercial history (under new regulations property owners in the four-block retail precinct are required to submit plans for 7500-square metre parcels of land). Australian architect Timothy Moore warns against an emerging 'corporate urbanism' turning the CBD into a 'suburban business park.' Can the next generation of buildings, he asks, 'deliver the social diversity, environmental sustainability and sense of place that a great 21st-century city needs?'[11]

5. There should be a place where only the things you want to happen, happen. — *Where the Wild Things Are*

Thanks for the memory, say some, but the transitional movement can move on. It's served its purpose. Now it's time to get serious. But the experimental, the propositional, the occupying momentum that has grown in Christchurch since the earthquake, says editor and writer Barnaby Bennett, 'is what makes Christchurch a unique place at the moment. It is what brings all these little moments of life to the city. And great cultural cities do these things — if we want Christchurch to be a good city, this is what we need.'[12]

Others agree. According to *The Guardian*, Gap Filler's 'commitment to community engagement is shaping the future of the city.'[13] In 2013 *Lonely Planet* named Christchurch one of the world's Top 10 Cities to Visit. 'There's a sense of energy in Christchurch,' it wrote, 'that is informing and inspiring the city's renewal.'[14] 'The city is experiencing a rebirth with creativity and wit,' *The New York Times* chimed in. 'Though much of the central city has yet to be rebuilt, entrepreneurs and volunteers are finding surprising ways to make temporary use of empty lots and bring life back to the downtown.'[15]

The unplanned interlude—between the immediate devastation and the emergence of a new, slickly marketed rebuilt city—has given time for the belief in more widespread participation in city-making processes to take root, shifting the transitional into a more permanent force, reigniting a sense of ownership and personal and social investment.

On the evening of 20 October 2012 a stretch of Gloucester St in downtown Christchurch, previously within the no-go confines of the inner-city red zone, seethed with people, music, light and energy. Luxcity, the inaugural Festival of Transitional Architecture (FESTA), drew over 20,000 Cantabrians into the city in an unprecedented act of re-ownership. Repeated in 2013 and 2014, FESTA is a provocative, anarchic form of creative experimentation.

In a city ruptured not only by earthquakes but also by 'National Corporate master planning', such initiatives, writes Parker, can restore a sense of place by reoccupying and reimagining a broken city 'with a view to proposing new collaborative projects that interrupt a mindset rooted in the ideological fantasies of late neo-liberalism.'[16]

From an arts perspective, he says, 'Christchurch has always been seen as a conservative place but in many places that are conservative you have people fighting against that—this wonderful angry passionate desire for something else. When the earthquake happened those on the periphery suddenly had a place in the centre. Now the city has this potential to be this experimental avant garde place. A conversation has begun and now it's about keeping those conversations going.'[17]

6. And above all, watch with glittering eyes the whole world around you. — *Roald Dahl*

Christchurch, New Zealand, 2016. Our initial circumnavigation of the cordon, our unbelieving gaze, has changed. Where once we failed to absorb, we now scrutinise. Where once we stared, we now watch. As long-awaited insurance monies, private and public investment and business confidence shape the foundations of large-scale inner city constructions, that scrutiny is becoming more critical. In 2013 Gap Filler co-founder Andrew Just and Venezuelan architect Alejandro Haiek Coll, co-director of design collective LabProFab, designed the Grandstandium, a 30-seat mobile viewing platform complete with binoculars and a commentator box, recently used to draw attention to and provoke discussion on, new steps in the city's 'recovery'. Public protests against the proposed demolition of the the Christchurch Town Hall, designed by Miles Warren and Maurice Mahoney, and the reconfiguration of the historic Victoria Square have been successful.

In 2015, editors of *Once in a Lifetime: City-building after Disaster in Christchurch* organised a 'recovery clinic' in an inner city bar to discuss the Government's Draft Transition Recovery Plan for the gradual transfer of control of the city rebuild from the government to local authorities. In a resurrection of the participatory process of the council-run Share-an-Idea project, the *Press* launched 'A Great Place to Be', calling on Christchurch residents to submit their priorities for the future city. Public engagement in the city, our city, has been fanned. People care. They are part of the conversation.

'That is the power of the transitional,' says Halliday. 'It is grassroots, bubble up. It hasn't come from government. It's coming from fellow citizens, it's coming from us.'

Not for everyone, of course. Some avoid the inner city — too raw, too chaotic. Some are still mired in battles related to their own homes and neighbourhoods. But for a city that has lost so much, decisions about the shape of the emerging city will not be easily surrendered. Even as the city's gaps close, as toadstool chairs and pallet constructions are replaced by more permanent structures, there is the hope at least that this post-quake history of urban revitalisation, as borne out by a peripatetic dance floor, a sound garden, a book exchange, a community garden, has established a habit of engagement that will endure.

7. There's no place like home. — *Dorothy*

A sense of place is inevitably tied to the natural environment. For Christchurch it is the braided river, the Southern Alps, the Port Hills, the nor'westers, the Canterbury light. 'And that constant sense of surprise,' says Halliday, 'when you cross over the Port Hills and see Lyttelton Harbour.' Changes here are slow: the gradual shift from grazing to dairy, the loss of shelter belts, the subtle movements of the path of the Waimakariri. In the city centre the physical changes to Christchurch's identity have been more abrupt. The architectural legacy defined by Warren and Mahoney — concrete block, exposed concrete beams, pitched roof — is being replaced by large edifices of glass and steel. Where once whole streets told the story of the city's Victorian and Edwardian architectural past, now only pockets of heritage buildings remain. A sense of disconnection was inevitable but there is also hope, excitement in the potential of a not-entirely planned new city stumbling out of the dust and the clamour and the levelling truth of the commercial and civic balance sheet. Already a rash of books and calendars and photographic displays showing the 'lost heritage' of 'old Christchurch' look faded, antiquated.

Will we find a 'there' here?

Urban sociologists and geographers read space not as a bounded locale or territory, but as a social production, informed by historic social and cultural activity, defined by the lived experiences and identifications of its people. It is an imaginary space, changing, growing, giving form to personal or group identity and that deep sense of place, of *there*. Such experiences are held within the physical forms of a cityscape that continue to grow and change in accordance not with a masterplan but with the evolving needs of its residents. As architect and design critic Edwin Heathcote says, the city remains 'stubbornly resistant to perfection'.[18] Ideal is not that interesting; incoherence is good.

Within the current contradiction of broken buildings, new glass-clad structures and large tracts of levelled land, a new urban landscape is taking form. A more uncertain, less predictable city. The aspirations of the city blueprint have lost their hard-edged perfection. The high-amped energy of the transitional movement has become more muted. But in the cracks in the planning there is the possibility of more voices being heard, of more and different experiences shaping the personal and collective associations that formalise our connections with the shared space of the city.

'We are no longer defined by the void or by irreconcilable scenes of destruction,' says Halliday, 'but by anarchic creativity, by Edible Canterbury, by the mountain-biking proposal on the Port Hills. It is a mistake not to make [the city] as rich as you possibly can, as long as it feels like we still own it — that it's mine, it belongs to me, I belong to it.'

Subheadings:

1   From *Alice's Adventures in Wonderland* by Lewis Carroll
2   From *The House at Pooh Corner* by A.A. Milne
3   From *Alice's Adventures in Wonderland* by Lewis Carroll
4   From *Oh, the Places You'll Go* by Dr Seuss
5   From *Where the Wild Things Are* (2009 film directed by Spike Jonze)
6   From *The Minpins* by Roald Dahl
7   From *The Wizard of Oz* by Frank Baum

Notes on Sources:

1   Qtd in Matt Werner, 'Gertrude Stein's Oakland', *Huffington Post*, 31 July 2012, accessed 1 July 2015, http://www.huffingtonpost.com/matt-werner/oakland-in-popular-memory_b_1560227.html.
2   Kelly Baker, 'Identity, Memory and Place', *The Word Hoard* (2012), accessed 1 August 2015, http://ir.lib.uwo.ca/cgi/viewcontent.cgi?article=1003&context=wordhoard.
3   Fiona Farrell, *The Villa at the Edge of Empire* (Auckland: Penguin Random House, 2015), 104.
4   Glenn Albrecht, 'The age of solastalgia', *The Conversation* (2012), accessed 29 July 2015, http://theconversation.com/the-age-of-solastalgia-8337.
5   Jessica Halliday, interview, 6 July 2015. Subsequent references to Halliday also taken from this source.
6   Ryan Reynolds, interview, 14 May 2015. Subsequent references to Ryan Reynolds also taken from this source.
7   Coralie Win, interview, 21 January 2015.
8   Richard Reynolds, qtd in *Big Smoke*, 'A City of Bars and Railings', Big Smoke (2011), accessed 12 July 2015, http://www.bigsmoke.org.uk/?p=11289.

9   Christchurch City Council, *Draft Central City Recovery Plan for Ministerial Approval* (Christchurch: CCC, 2011), iv.

10   George Parker, interview, 13 June 2015.

11   Timothy Moore, '"Bland corporate urbanism" taking over central Christchurch', *The Press*, 27 November 2015, 15.

12   Barnaby Bennett, interview, 2 February 2015.

13   Laura Zabel, 'Six creative ways artists can improve communities', *The Guardian*, 12 February 2015, accessed 12 July 2015, http://www.theguardian.com/culture-professionals-network/2015/feb/12/creative-ways-artists-improve-communities.

14   Brett Atkinson, 'Christchurch revival: why New Zealand's comeback city is a must-see for 2013', 25 October, accessed 12 July 2015, http://www.lonelyplanet.com/new-zealand/christchurch-and-canterbury/christchurch/travel-tips-and-articles/77531.

15   Justin Bergman, '52 Places to Go in 2014', *New York Times*, 5 September 2014, accessed 12 July 2015, http://www.nytimes.com/interactive/2014/01/10/travel/2014-places-to-go.html?_r=0.

16   George Parker, 'Place-making or place-faking?: the River and the City in Canterbury Tales', unpublished thesis, accessed 1 November, 2015, http://www.freetheatre.org.nz/uploads/1/1/1/0/11101030/george_parker_adsa_paper_of_ct_2014_.pdf.

17   George Parker, interview, 13 June 2015.

18   Edwin Heathcote, 'Urban Outfitters', *Financial Times*, 29 June 2007, accessed 12 July 2015, http://www.ft.com/intl/cms/s/0/802b8c86-26a6-11dc-8e18-000b5df10621.html#axzz3htCx6P44.

Sally Blundell is a journalist, researcher and essayist living in Christchurch. She has written for a number of magazines and journals and currently works for the *NZ Listener*. She edited *Look This Way: New Zealand Writers on New Zealand Artists* (Auckland University Press, 2007), which was shortlisted for the New Zealand Book Awards. Her doctoral research at the University of Canterbury looks at the role of speech and speechlessness in literary portrayals of trauma. She currently writes on art, architecture, heritage, trade and, in the wake of the Canterbury earthquakes, urban design. Her writing has explored the 'environmental amnesia' that afflicted Christchurch before the 2010 and 2011 earthquakes, the role of South Island iwi Ngāi Tahu in the city rebuild and the rediscovery of a social and ecological past. She contributed to *Once in a Lifetime: City-Building after Disaster in Christchurch* (Freerange Press, 2014).

Underwater Reach

Cherie Lacey

I

I was halfway through my psychoanalytic training when I made this return home, the cost of the airfare from Melbourne to Napier constituting my official Christmas present from my parents. Flying above Napier airport, if you know what you're looking for, you can make out the ground that was raised up after the 1931 earthquake. This one event caused large areas of land to be hauled up from beneath the water, filling in sections of the coastline from Bay View in the north to Te Awanga in the south. From the air, it's possible to trace out the old inner harbour, once called Ahuriri Lagoon, and the original internal shoreline. The Napier airport is built on a section of reclaimed land that was once the lagoon floor.

The paddocks surrounding the airport have recently been opened up to the public and a bike track built through it, which weaves around the back of the airport and follows the old shoreline into Napier city. Over the years various owners have tried, unsuccessfully, to turn it into productive farmland, only to find its combination of wetlands and estuarine saltmarsh interspersed with paddock unable to support productive livestock. For most people it's a place to pass through or fly over rather than dwell on. The Melbourne boyfriend once said, *It looks like rural Victoria*. But it only looks this way from a distance.

If you go to the local museum you can find personal accounts that communicate the shock of seeing this land appear in the moments following the quake. One audio item provides an account by a man called Gordon Amner, who was a young farmhand in 1931. He recalls how, in the moments after the quake, he climbed the hills and looked out to sea, fearing a tsunami. The sea did retreat, he says, but it did so permanently. In the lagoon where he used to sail boats there were now piles of dead fish and exposed horse mussels. The museum says that the earthquake 'gifted' Napier with more than 2000 hectares of new land.

My parents' house sits on the beach in front of the airport. On this visit home, one night over a whiskey, Dad told me that old Napier was buried behind their house. This is the language he uses sometimes, dropped into conversation just like that. *They buried Napier behind our house.* He was telling me how he takes his grandson, my brother's boy, out there to dig for treasures—old bottles, ceramics and other debris that was removed from the town after the quake. Not knowing where else to put it, the city councillors ordered the debris to be dumped on the reclaimed land and covered with soil, helping to shore it up. You don't have to dig too far before you find some of these old objects, and a bad storm will sometimes do the work for you. My nephew keeps these artefacts, his treasures, on the top of his set of drawers, still dirty but carefully lined up in a row. I asked Dad if we could go for a walk there the next day.

I wanted to talk. I wanted him to help me work out what to do next with my training, which wasn't, truth be told, working out all that well. Being in this place has always functioned for me as a kind of interval, parentheses marking the shift from one chapter in my life to another.

The process of becoming a psychoanalyst is a drawn-out and expensive one, requiring about four years of daily sessions and academic study, plus attendance at regular clinical seminars, supervision and research projects. Despite the impracticality of the training, I was fascinated by the notion of the unconscious—'that inner foreign country, foreign home, country of lost countries', as Helene Cixous has called it.[1] I was taken by the notion that we're not always conscious of that which affects us, that the words of others can become inscribed in us. This is a kind of writing, I was taught, one that exists in the place of the unconscious, as the unconscious. Sometimes, words become permanent marks, altering us completely. At other times the writing isn't permanent and eventually fades away, eroding in time.

'The psychoanalytic training isn't really working,' I told Dad.

'What do you talk about?'

'Mostly just memories—my childhood or when I was a teenager,' I told him. 'Sometimes, I talk about what happened the day before.'

'There are times that I have nothing to say,' I told him, 'but feel the expectation so I just see what comes out.'

'Sometimes, it's not even about the talking. One day, my bike got a flat tyre when I was on my way to a session. I called my analyst to say that I wouldn't make it on time because I had to change the tyre. She said not to bother coming in at all.'

'She told me at the next session that I would have to pay for the one I missed because I was *acting out*. The flattie was a "resistance to the treatment", so she would charge for it.'

Dad balked at this, and questioned my analyst's qualifications and the whole economic enterprise of it.

I continued: 'Anyway, I don't think I believe in it anymore.'

Psychoanalysis requires a kind of faith in order for it to work, if it ever does work. Maybe this is one of the reasons psychoanalytic groups resemble religious groups, cults even. This has been commented on by a number of people, including some of psychoanalysis's eminent practitioners.

We made our way across the soggy paddocks, shallow ponds crossed with thin dirt pathways where it's possible to walk but you have to pay attention. Twice, light planes on an intermittent provincial schedule pass overhead. I'd never seen anyone else walk through here. Now that I thought about it, I wasn't even sure this was public land.

In my dreams, at this time, I was always trying to run without shoes on.

As we walked on, my narrative became a bit more demanding. 'What do you think I should do?' I wanted to be told, I think, since there was no *me* there anymore, at least not one capable of action. 'Subjective destitution' is the psychoanalytic term for this, and denotes the psychic state where the ego, the *I*, dissolves. In the course of treatment, this is a necessary state to achieve before you can pass to the position of the analyst. That's how it's referred to in psychoanalytic circles—you pass to a different position, undergo the pass, make the pass. *Has she made the pass?* I would sometimes overhear at a function, a topic of hushed gossip. It means that you're no longer invested in the *I*, or no longer think that you're the same as the *I* who writes or speaks about yourself.

Dad eventually changed the subject. He talked instead about the history of the particular section of land we were walking through. Not the post-earthquake burials, but the history of Māori inhabitation and movements.

A local history enthusiast, Dad's bookshelves are lined with small-press publications about Hawkes Bay. Across the flat land that used to be the lagoon is a large hill. We walked towards it and Dad told me that its name is Roro-o-Kuri, 'Brain of the Dog', so called because once when a respected chief visited the hapū they cooked a dog for the celebrations and gave the brains to the chief to eat. It used to be an island surrounded by the lagoon. I learnt that a taniwha lived in a cave within the lagoon, and would ride out to sea through a small outlet, which is about where my parents' house sits now. The lagoon was a major source of food for the people of Roro-o-Kuri, Dad said, and at the base of the hill he showed me how the ground is made up of layers of shells where cockles and other foods were prepared before being taken up to the pā.

I'd never heard it called Roro-o-Kuri before. In my family, we usually refer to the hill as *Good News Mountain*, or its alternative name, *Boring News Mountain* (I can no longer remember what we called it before we adopted these appellations). Both names were bestowed by my nephew, the treasure hunter. The 'good news' refers to the time my dad took him up the hill and told him that his dad was coming home to live after working for a couple of years in the Western Australian mines. The other title refers to the times my dad tried to pass on the area's pre-colonial history to the seven-year-old.

It started to rain and so we circled back towards the house. The ground here is already soft, and rivulets of water soon formed on the surface, washing away the smaller fragments of shells. In our haste to get back under cover we forgot about looking for the remnants of old Napier.

Later that night, I browsed old maps of Napier online and read about reclaimed land. I found out that the word 'reclamation' comes from 'the action of claiming or demanding'. Usually, reclaiming land is a manmade process, making new land available for efficient, economic use. In this case, areas of water are filled in with rock or cement, and then covered with clay and dirt until it reaches the desired height. Less often, reclamation is the result of a sudden natural event like an earthquake, the land making its own demands on the sea. Either way, by natural force or conscious action, change happens.

II

Ahuriri Lagoon: the land was always there, under the water. Except it wasn't really, it was something entirely different—a Taniwha's cave and bed of horse mussels. Repetition isn't the same as history, nor is it the return of the past; the first time it appears, repetition is already repetition. I tend to think of the essay as a kind of repetition, signalling the presence of an unmarked encounter, an experience that was originally missed.

III

The bike that I used to ride in Melbourne is now in the shed at home in Wellington, an artefact of my old life. It's a vintage Peugeot mixte—white frame, tan leather accessories, painstakingly retrofitted with chrome attachments bought online from eBay France. Despite not being a cyclist I'd been persuaded to get one by the Melbourne boyfriend, a true cycling enthusiast. He'd thought and thought about it, he said, about which bike suited me best, and came up with this: a vintage Peugeot mixte.

I rode this bike around Melbourne for a year before I came back to New Zealand, and I couldn't part with it when I left. It was the way I related to that city. I learnt how to get from the northern suburbs into the city centre passing through back roads and laneways, and how you can ride along the Yarra River cycle track instead of braving the main roads. The bike looks comically out of place now. It leans precariously against our woodpile, and both my husband and I curse it every time we go to collect wood for the fire. You have to balance the bike with one hand while trying to gather together logs in the other, scooping them into the crook of your arm.

It can be a relief to be handed particular words and told, *That's you*. Sometimes the words fit, and sometimes not—usually this process doesn't cause too much grief. But it can become more complicated when the words appear in the guise of the most familiar part of yourself, when they seem to come from the inner reaches, like the unconscious, or love. This fits the theory: in Melbourne, I was taught that I'm not the author of my own text. *You are a poem*, I was told, *but not the poet* (I cringe now that I come to write it down). The only freedom to be had is in signing your name to the text, assuming it as your own.

I had spent two years reconstructing a narrative of place—family, memories, scenes—with my analyst in Melbourne. She would seize upon particular words as especially important, and I—thinking they must hold the key to something—would duly respond, uncovering the memory further, digging deeper. *We are not the authors of our own text*, she said.

This text-that-was-not-my-own didn't work when it was overlaid on this place. It demanded a different story be made, one that included dog's brains and a taniwha and a buried lagoon, an earthquake, shards of ceramic and the complicated life of a family. I write about this place as a way of reclaiming it, not as possession or appropriation, but—quite literally—as a text for which it's possible for me to be the author, since this is a place that exists only for me, as me.

Sometimes, I think, words become enduring inscriptions, an event causing permanent upheaval, and other times they don't, like rain falling on soft ground.

Notes on sources:

1   Helene Cixous, *Three Steps on the Ladder of Writing* (New York: Columbia University Press, 1993), 70.

Cherie Lacey received her PhD (film) from the University of Auckland and MA (literature) from Victoria University of Wellington. Her research explores the ways in which place affects our psyche, drawing primarily from psychoanalytic and postcolonial theory. More recently, she has approached these ideas through creative nonfiction writing, and is currently based at the International Institute of Modern Letters (Victoria University of Wellington), where she is writing a memoir of a failed psychoanalysis. Cherie also lectures in media studies at Victoria University of Wellington.

Chop Suey Patties and Histories of Place

Tony Ballantyne

I have been going to Fairways takeaways in Caversham in southern Dunedin since it opened in 1977 or 1978, when I was five or six years old. Prior to that my family mainly went to the chip shop we called 'Fatty's' further down South Road, the main road that runs through Caversham. We called it 'Fatty's' because the owner was fuller figured than the other Chinese New Zealanders who ran the local chip shops and also because they sold chips that were really fat, like a good-sized potato cleaved in four and then deep-fried. My mum and I shifted allegiances to Fairways when they opened up though: they had (and still have) really crisp crinkle-cut chips, and my Mum loved their spring rolls. Mum and I would normally stop on the way home from either my rugby or cricket practice on a Thursday night to get 'greasies', as she called them; my Dad, who worked night shifts, missed out.

After our family moved from Caversham to another south Dunedin suburb, St Kilda, in 1987, we would still sometimes go back to Fairways. And when I flatted in Caversham during my 1993 honours year at Otago University and in the following year as I prepared to go to England to do my PhD, my girlfriend Sally and I would sometimes get Fairways, although she initially preferred another local place called Golden Chips. We returned to Dunedin in 2002 and have lived in Kew, immediately southeast of Caversham, since 2008. A feed from Fairways often marks the end of the week, the end of a school term or a good achievement at school for our kids: fish and chips are a part of the routines of our family life.

But for me, as a historian, Fairways has additional significance: it is a site that has been a spur to my thinking about the meanings of place and community. In my writing I advocate the primacy of archives and the power of archival research to generate new historical understanding and interpretations. The shaping of historical argument is, however, an imaginative and creative process where the historian's knowledge of the past gained through an extensive reading of primary sources is drawn into interplay with their knowledge of the relevant scholarly literatures and the pressing intellectual, cultural and political questions of the historian's own time. The individual sensibility of the historian is very important in ordering their priorities, generating ideas and inflecting their arguments.

My own sense of attachment to Caversham has undoubtedly shaped my work in a variety of ways and has been a key driver of my dissatisfaction with histories that dwell on the imagined national community without grappling with the specificities of individual places, including their particular connections beyond New Zealand. I am quite conscious, for example, that Caversham was in my mind when Brian Moloughney and I began to explore the imprint of connections to Asia in shaping the cultural development of colonial Otago. At one level, the spur to that work was co-teaching world history, which saw us grappling with long histories of cross-cultural engagement and readings, such as Donald Lach's landmark series *Asia in the Making of Europe*, which stressed the constitutive place of India, China, Japan and Southeast Asia in the development of European languages, cultures and thought during the early modern period. Brian, an expert on Chinese history, and I also shared an interest in the work of the missionary Alexander Don and the 'roll' of Chinese he assembled during his itinerant work within Otago and Southland from the 1880s. But in many ways my interest in the imprint of Asia in the south was largely motivated by my experience of growing up in Caversham with its prominent families of Chinese descent who shaped its commercial life. I knew that such families had played an important role in shaping the development of south Dunedin more generally and I knew many of their shops—primarily takeaways and fruiterers. I had gone to school with kids from these families and, like my siblings, had played sport with and against these children. I also remembered the pleasure my mum took in buying vegetables from Quuns Fruiterers in Caversham that she couldn't grow in her own rudimentary garden; she loved their courgettes, beans and Chinese cabbage. And, of course, there was Fairways, with its chow meins, stirfries, foo youngs and sweet and sour dishes, as well as its spring rolls and chop suey patties that were indicative of the profound localisation of Cantonese culinary traditions. This cultural interweaving was very common in Dunedin and the south more generally from the 1950s and it marked these takeaway establishments off from the resolutely European traditions that characterised the food and culture of fish and chip shops across the United Kingdom from their emergence in the late 19th century.

Brian and I ended up writing an essay called 'Asia in Murihiku', which attempted to recover the broad imprint of Asian people and things in southern New Zealand. We argued that this material suggested that it was important to prise open inward-looking national and nationalistic narratives and return New Zealand histories to the broader cultural fields and economic networks that conditioned their development. One key point we made was the importance of thinking 'below' the nation, exploring local patterns of socio-economic development and taking the weight of regional structures and cultural patterns seriously. That commitment to thinking both below and beyond the nation has become fundamental to my research.

I returned to these issues late in 2008 when our family returned to Dunedin after a brief period living in the United States. We purchased a house in Kew, the suburb adjacent to Caversham. We began to spend more time in Cavy and started getting fish and chips from Fairways again. At this stage I had really committed to working on the history of Otago and Southland and was particularly doing a lot of work on Gore, in part because there were especially rich manuscript holdings for the town's history but also because two very good newspapers served Gore district—the *Southern Standard* and the *Mataura Ensign*—which were an excellent foundation for research.

One thing that struck me as I worked through those newspapers was the abiding centrality of public works in the politics of Gore district: roads, railways, ferries and bridges stood at the heart of Gore's often fraught politics. When I was initially reading those newspapers I tended to skim these discussions of infrastructure, focusing instead on intellectual debates and the development of local cultural institutions such as libraries, athenaeums, and schools as they were the primary focus of my research. Slowly it dawned on me, however, that there were strong connections between public works and cultural life and that those relationships need to be thought about.

Fairways was, in part, a spur to that understanding. On Friday nights I make our order: Sally, who is now my wife, prefers a spring roll, my daughters Evie and Clara have the same thing, a battered hot dog each and a sausage, which they share. I have a sausage and a chop suey patty—a true southern delicacy of finely shredded veges and onion, deep-fried in a disc of batter; $1.50 of pure pleasure. Then my habit is to lean against the old *Indiana Jones* pinball machine in the corner and look east through the plate glass window to watch the traffic on South Road. Across the road is the main strip of Caversham shops. They are a dismal sight now, mostly abandoned, sitting under a rusty, dilapidated and sagging light-brown corrugated iron verandah. As a child I would walk along past those shops on the way to school: past the stationery shop and newsagents at the start of the row, Quun's impressive fruiterers (which had bright displays of fruit, vegetables and flowers spilling out onto the footpath), the Caversham bakery (which sold fresh bread and fat cream buns), the Tuck Inn (a takeaway place that was well-known for both its burgers and arcade of pinball machines and videogames), and then finally past Harper's drapers. In my memory, in the late 1970s the shopping centre was busy with people from early in the morning through until after 5pm. Even on a Thursday night it would be often hard to get a park near Fairways on the way home. But things are very different now and my visits to Fairways over the past seven years have made me think a lot about decay and the erosion of community.

Perhaps in 2006 or 2007 I read the British geographer Doreen Massey's book *For Space*, and reading that book in turn lead me to her earlier landmark essay 'A Global Sense of Place'. The essay used Kilburn High Road in London to emphasise the centrality of connections in shaping places, pressing against readings of places as self-sufficient, enclosed, clearly bounded. That argument resonated with me in light of my own earlier work, which emphasises the importance of global imperial networks in shaping the development of various colonial communities, and it confirmed the argument that I had developed with Brian Moloughney about the importance of Asia, especially China, in the shaping of 19th-century Otago and Southland.

But it was on looking out on the intermittent traffic of South Road and the rundown shops that I really understood the weight of Massey's arguments. Her work underscored that places are unique not only as a result of their topography and demography but because they are in process. She argued that places can be usefully understood as points of convergence, where particular pathways, networks, peoples in motion and sets of social relationships intersect. Places are unique not only as a result of their topography and demography but because they are a specific point where a unique set of networks, movements and exchanges intersect. The changing shape of these convergences remake communities, giving places their distinctive character. Thinking about the depressing view through the window of Fairways, I was struck by the idea that Caversham had unwound and that its once bustling commercial and social life had almost died away. Caversham's decline, the slow unravelling that I had witnessed over three decades, made knots seem an obvious metaphor for the nature of place.

In an essay 'On Place, Space and Mobility in Nineteenth-Century New Zealand' I drew on Massey (whom I openly acknowledged) and the thoughts that occurred to me in Fairways (which I didn't mention) to argue:

> we might think of places as knot-like conjunctures where the ceaseless small-scale mobilities of life in the location interlocked into the more extensive networks that enabled the regular movement of people, things and words in and out of the location. The shape of the knots shifted—as new networks developed, old linkages declined and the relative significance of various connections oscillated—they changed, they were dependent on time.

This argument still guides much of my thinking on the histories of our islands, but as I completed the essay I had some nagging doubts. I had committed myself to the idea of always arguing upwards from the archive. But while this argument about the integral role of mobility and connections in shaping community illuminated many things I found in my sources, I was always a little dissatisfied that it felt like a higher-level characterisation of those processes rather than being firmly anchored in a specific source.

Those concerns eventually evaporated when I was working back through my notes on the *Mataura Ensign* and came across my transcription of a remarkable essay published on 11 July 1884. The original essay had been presented two days before its publication to the Gore Literary and Debating Society by Archibald Fletcher, a solicitor and the Town Clerk of Gore. Fletcher, a man known for his 'luminous intellect', explored the subject of 'The Local Press', stressing the elevating nature of literacy and the power of the newspaper as a progressive engine of social transformation. But what was particularly striking about his arguments was his interest in the connections between the materiality of the newspaper and the cultural work of reading. He noted that the printing press transformed paper, which is 'gradually drawn in, goes winding around, and flies off at the other side where it is received, no longer white, but spotted with letters, dotted with words, and pregnant with ideas.' These ideas were produced, embedded and circulated within expansive communication networks, including the telegraph, the steam engine and steamer. The contemporary newspaper was an artefact that reflected a world encompassed by an increasingly dense mesh of networks that meant that readers in Gore were firmly linked to distant lands, contemporary developments and new ideas:

> the newsboy melodiously sings—'The MATAURA ENSIGN, only three-pence,' and so for the smallest silver coin that circulates in the colony we are able to read on what was last week tussock grass and this week solution in the mill, but to-day firm paper, an epitome of the words spoken yesterday, 12,000 miles away, by the most august sovereign in the world!

How did this connect back to Caversham? I realised these colonial newspapers recorded the dynamics of community formation, while Cavy's built environment was a kind of archive too, a sad repository that documented decline and disconnection. With a shrinking population and few economic opportunities, it has not been redeveloped, gentrification is a very distant prospect, and this means that its shabby shops stand as an unintended archive which records a past that might be recoverable to the historian or the geographer, but which the community itself cannot restore.

Why has Caversham unravelled and how might this historical argument about the primacy of connections and mobility in shaping places of the past illuminate the present of places like Cavy? Much of Caversham's decline can be narrated as a story of post-industrial decay. Central to the suburb's development in the late 19th century were a host of small workshops within the neighbourhood—boot makers, tailors, carpenters and joiners, and small metalworking firms—as well as the larger industrial sites in nearby parts of south Dunedin, such as the gasworks and especially Hillside Workshops. A range of food and beverage producers, grocery stores and retailers developed to support the suburb's rapidly growing and densely settled population. A complex matrix of social institutions—schools, churches, lodges, clubs and associations of various kinds—laced people together, bringing the families of labourers, the semi-skilled and skilled workers, and proprietors together in a range of social settings, underpinning a robust political culture that was energised by various denominational traditions, labour politics and social reform movements, including first-wave feminism.

As the century progressed, however, the economic base of the community was slowly transformed with new technologies, reorganising methods of production and scaling back the size of the industrial workforce. When my parents moved to Caversham in 1949 it was still a robust community where middle-class and working-class families lived in close proximity and were firmly linked through sports, religion, and a mesh of local shops and clubs. But decline firmly set in during the 1960s and 1970s, as the remaining small workshops closed and larger factories came under pressure, cutting their workforces. The hollowing out of Caversham's economic base has been protracted and painful. The fate of Hillside Workshops is emblematic: over 1200 men had once worked producing and repairing locomotives and rolling stock; by 2012 its staff had been reduced to 115. KiwiRail's major contract with China CNR Corporation for the production of 300 flat-deck container wagons in that year effectively marked the culmination of the erosion of Dunedin's industrial capacity, a stark reversal from the 1890s when the city had a vibrant engineering sector and was the nation's industrial heart. The closing of factories and a seemingly unending sequence of job losses in turn sapped the vitality of Caversham's commercial centre and transformed the demographics of the neighbourhood. Caversham is now the poorest part of south Dunedin, which itself is one of the most impoverished urban areas in our country. In class terms, the neighbourhood has become homogeneous, with many families dependent on low-paid casual work or welfare, while becoming more ethnically diverse as its population of Māori, Pasifika and new migrant families has grown significantly.

But the unravelling of Caversham is also a story about infrastructure and transportation. It is a direct outcome of a decision in the 1970s to build a new motorway that rerouted State Highway 1 so that it bypassed Caversham, allowing articulated trucks, especially those carrying woodchips and logs to Port Chalmers, faster passage through Dunedin's southern outskirts. The Dunedin City Planning Department welcomed this, as it had long been concerned about congestion in the Caversham shopping area. From the creation of the state highway system in 1936, State Highway 1 had run directly through Caversham: South Road was State Highway 1 and functioned as the main route in and out of the city. A 1973 Planning Department report, *Caversham: Objectives For Redevelopment*, noted that South Road carried, on average, an excess of 13,000 vehicles per day and could look forward to the reduction of that traffic to around 4,300 vehicles—a change that would render the traffic flow more efficient, relieve pressure on parking and make the bustling shopping centre more aesthetically pleasing. What the planners did not fully foresee were the economic and social consequences that flowed from the rerouting of traffic with the construction of the new motorway. Within a decade or so, the vitality had been sucked out of the neighbourhood's centre and many of its shops were abandoned.

When I go to Fairway takeaways on a Friday night now, Cavy is a sad place. There isn't much traffic compared to steady flows of the 1970s. Cars drive through on their way home or into town, but not many stop. Some do pull into Mitchell's Tavern, the pub that is Caversham's most vibrant business, or the Four Square, which is still run by one branch of the Shum family. Fairways does a good trade, especially on Friday and Saturday nights, but they have little competition now and it's always easy to get a park right outside, which wasn't the case a generation ago. The derelict shops you see across the road and the other marginal businesses that remain demonstrate how Caversham is clearly a place that has been partially unmade by the loss of traffic; it really does seem to be coming apart.

But why should anyone outside the neighbourhood or beyond Dunedin care? Caversham, and places like it, prompt us to think differently about histories of New Zealand by reckoning with decline, disintegration and failure. New Zealand history is typically emplotted as a story of progress and advancement, typically ordered around three positive narrative arcs: the emergence and elaboration of a progressive state; cross-cultural engagements, accommodations and the resolution of conflicts between Māori and Pākehā; and the slow development of national identity. These forms of narration tend to produce an abstracted and placeless vision of the past—these are histories of the state, of social values, of national identity—all things that tend to be disconnected from the actual places within which people love, work, build families, fashion institutions and engage in conflict, and identify strongly with through the routines of social life and the work of narrative and memory. Keith Sinclair, of course, was the great champion and architect of national history from the late 1950s. He believed that a generation of pedants was needed to assemble the building blocks of an authentic, self-contained and self-confident national history. He imagined the national story as a conscious process of building something or completing a puzzle. In this view, places were only important insofar as they were pieces of the national whole; unless they were slotted into that bigger story they were really useless and meaningless fragments.

But actually taking localities seriously, understanding them not as fragments or microcosms of the nation, but as the sites from where people actually live their lives and construct their worlds, strikes me as a fundamentally important cultural and political project. And thinking about and through places like

65

Caversham opens up vantage points and narrative arcs that are very different from our national-history tradition, with its liberal optimism and its celebration of the 'good-hearted' national character (something that underpinned Michael King's popular *Penguin History of New Zealand*).

Caversham's transformation also has a particular significance for how we think about equality and inequality. The suburb is very prominent in *An Accidental Utopia?: Social Mobility and the Foundations of an Egalitarian Society, 1880–1940* by Erik Olssen, Clyde Griffen and Frank Jones, a vital but largely overlooked study of the genesis and operation of equality in an earlier moment in our nation's history. Olssen and his co-authors explored the centrality of three forms of mobility—marital, work-life and intergenerational—in shaping south Dunedin's class structure and cultural pattern. They emphasised how the absence of residential segregation on class lines, marriage between families of different economic standing, the power and influence of unions and social reform movements, and the operation of open social institutions—schools, churches and clubs—enabled the people of Caversham and south Dunedin to fashion a social and economic world that was more egalitarian in economic terms than the Old World communities of the United Kingdom and Ireland, from which they had migrated. So the history of places like Caversham are key to understanding the specific circumstances and practices that help establish equality as a real feature of life in New Zealand, just as we might use the suburb to tell stories about post-industrial decline, the reorganisation of work and the consequences of disconnectedness in generating the deepening inequality of our contemporary moment. Thinking upwards from specific everyday sites—fish and chips shops like Fairways, for example—is essential if we are to grapple with the complexity of lived experience in these islands and, most importantly, if we are to fully countenance just how placed life is: the world seems profoundly different in Caversham than in Dunedin's more affluent suburbs like Maori Hill, let alone Wellington's Kelburn or Thorndon or Auckland's Parnell, Remuera or Takapuna.

Notes on Sources:

My essay with Brian Moloughney was published as 'Asia in Murihiku: Towards a Transnational History of Colonial Culture' in Moloughney and Ballantyne (eds.), *Disputed Histories: Imagining New Zealand's Pasts* (Otago: University of Otago Press, 2006), 65–92. My work on Gore includes: 'Reading the Newspaper in Colonial Otago', *Journal of New Zealand Studies*, 12 (2011), 47–63; 'On Place, Space and Mobility in Nineteenth Century New Zealand', *New Zealand Journal of History*, 45:1 (2011) and 'Thinking Local: Knowledge, Sociability and Community in Gore's Intellectual Life, 1875–1914', *New Zealand Journal of History*, 44:2 (2010), 138–56. The last two of these essays are anthologised, together with several other pieces that explore New Zealand historiography and the importance of place and connections, in my *Webs of Empire: Locating New Zealand's Colonial Past* (Wellington: Bridget Williams Books, 2012; North American edition: UBC Press, 2014). The development of my own interest in the past and my sensibility as a historian is the focus of my 'Paths to the Past' in Dane Kennedy and Antoinette Burton (eds.), *How Empire Shaped Us* (London: Bloomsbury Press, 2016). For the work of Doreen Massey, see her *For Space* (London: Sage Publications, 2006) and 'A Global Sense of Place', *Marxism Today*, 38 (1991), 24–9.

Tony Ballantyne is pro-vice-chancellor of Humanities at the University of Otago, where he is also a professor and director of the Centre for Research on Colonial Culture. He has published widely on the cultural history of the British Empire during the 19th century, as well as on colonial New Zealand. His latest work is *Entanglements of Empire: Missionaries, Māori and the Question of the Body* (Duke University Press, 2014; Auckland University Press, 2015). Much of his current scholarship focuses on the significance of place and region in the history of southern New Zealand.

Dirt

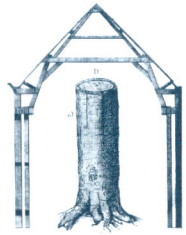

Lydia Wevers

When the Brancepeth library arrived at Victoria University in 1966, the librarians' principal emotion, as reported to me by one of them, was horror. Their horror was about dirt. At least half of its 2000 books are exceptionally dirty. They are filled with mud, dead insects and debris, and covered in a faded and often filthy red fabric known as 'linenette'. Wax dribbles, glass rings, food crusts and oily fingerprints are everywhere. Recently the special collections librarian, who manages the J.C. Beaglehole Room (where the library is held in its beautiful glass cases), told me that she also rejects things that are too dirty and she's not sure she would react differently if it arrived today. Opening the collection is, as Stephanie de Montalk found when she began sorting the archival papers of her cousin Count Geoffrey Potocki de Montalk, a threat to one's health. The Brancepeth library was established for the use of farm workers on the Wairarapa sheep station in the 1880s. For thirty years it operated as a subscription library before falling into disuse about the time of the First World War. It was gifted to Victoria in its original cases and is a very rare example of an intact and extant Victorian library which was not a personal collection. It is interesting as a material record of what Victorians, including working-class Victorians, actually read. When I started to research these questions, I realised that its dirt interested me. Dirt seemed to offer a response to Robert Darnton's well-known remark that we don't know enough about the 'where' of reading, and that the great mass of readers are lost in history but they leave their sweat and mud and food stains behind. When I followed the library to its original home on a sheep station in the Wairarapa it was apparent that dirt was an unavoidable and to some extent essential condition of the Historic Places Category 1 rating given to the whole site. Everything at Brancepeth was dirty. The old library building is crammed with objects and artefacts, like joiner's tools and old cooking utensils, from the late 19th century. The store is full of rusty tins and the tackle in the stables, with the original owners' names still attached, is cracked and buckled, old horse sweat in the seams. The records in the office, bound folios, released clouds of dead silverfish and dust every time I opened one. Piles of receipt books, letters, old accounts, posters, are everywhere. Every so often someone gives it a swish with a broom and the next time you come there's been a northerly and the office is full of leaves and dust. I hated eating my sandwiches in there.

You will notice my use of the first person. *Reading on the Farm*, my book about the Brancepeth library, is not a personal essay, but in it I use the first person and I regard it as a history of place. I was trying to write something like Emmanuel Le Roy Ladurie's *Montaillou*, a history of a village in France during the Plague, history with a narrow but deep focus, and when the layers and complications of the project began to tap me on the shoulder, I realised I had to put a boundary in place, a boundary of place. The books of the Brancepeth library carry place with them. I wanted them to form the basis of a history of place, a history which threw light on the people who interacted with those books, who moved and acted and made dirt in that place. Or only a little. Like other users of archives and other personal essayists I could only write about those books, their readers and this place as an embodied researcher, someone who read the books and put them back in their place. Even in their official home, the fourth floor of the university library, the books live in cases made from local timber by the joiner on the farm. Re-placing the Brancepeth library in its original home required me to spend a great deal of time there, especially in the station office, as the trust deed specifies that nothing shall leave the site. As I laboriously made my way through 14 years of station diaries and ledgers, a job which took me about five years, I developed a powerful and emotional relationship with the site, with its archives and with their dirt.

Antoinette Burton observes that the 'archive is a contact zone between past and present . . . the literal physical encounter with archives can have a profound effect on how one comes to understand and appreciate the histories they throw into bold relief'. I am focusing on dirt in this essay because it was the dirt of the Brancepeth books that opened, for me, a contact zone. I realised I couldn't make sense of these books, how they were used, how much they were read, their lives and the lives of the readers, without thinking about dirt, and to do that I had to take the dirt back to source.

Mary Louise Pratt's idea of the contact zone describes what Anne Salmond, talking about colonial encounter, has called 'between worlds'. While the collision of the past and the present is not exactly like violent intersections of different cultural and political worlds, it is similar in that it can never be fully understood. The past can only reveal itself to the present in snatches—forgotten objects, surviving buildings and artefacts, texts, memorials, and landscape traces. The history of place is always an act of reconstruction, an imaginative return. Who was here? How can I know them? In the case of Brancepeth I had various tools to help me. One of them is obviously the archival collections on the farm. The other is getting to know the fictional worlds Brancepeth readers entered by candlelight in a silent whare on a cold winter night.

One of the things I knew about the books is that they led travelling lives. Subscribers could request books to be sent out with food and other goods on bullock drays, which laboriously moved supplies around the boggy unmade roads of the farm. Library books were also read in the men's whare, in the shearing quarters, in the camps and outstations. They were read by fires, at the dinner table and in the grassy, muddy outdoors. Everywhere, the geography of the farm, 76,000 acres of Wairarapa eastern hill country, has left its residue on them. The dirtiness of the books, which could be 'read' as food, mud, oil, ash, insects, flowers, liquids, blood, possibly even translated as DNA, meant I started to think about the Brancepeth library as a contact zone between my present and these readers in the past. It seemed to me I could enter that past in some small way by thinking about the languages of place—paper, buildings, objects, landscape. And it was only through thinking about place that I could start to uncover some of the social and cultural layers of life in the 1890s. The mode in which to do this, I increasingly felt, was in a narrative that began with my presence as a reader of these grubby books and a visitor to the place they came from.

The Historic Places Category 1 site that is Brancepeth is imposing—a grand homestead with a turret, which you approach up a sweeping drive through a garden with a panoramic view towards the Tararua Range. If you turn right and don't go through the formal wooden entry gates, you come to the back way in; a rutted track leading to a cluster of outbuildings which includes the stables, the cookhouse, the chook house, the store library and the office. Class is written all over the site: one way for visitors and another for the diverse working population of the 1890s—bullockies; shepherds; roadmen; fencers. It wasn't till I went there that I realised how much the books too were stratified. The books that live in the special collections at Victoria University were used by everyone who could pay—actually only one-tenth of the whole work force paid to read them, though probably there was a penumbra of friends and family who also read the books. Inside the smoking room, gloomy even on a sunny day with its leather chairs, red velvet curtains, mounted antlers and portraits, there are the family books, many of which have tooled leather covers and gilt titles. They are mostly nonfiction, and interestingly almost all the New Zealand books live in the smoking room. These books are precious objects that did not travel outside the house. As I have written elsewhere, the books of the Brancepeth library, used by subscribers and run like a public library with a catalogue and housed in a separate building, are cheap, mass produced, glued, colonial editions and mostly popular fiction. Their cheapness is part of what reveals their relation to place—the paper is absorbent and tears easily, which means their spines are often broken and pages are missing, and the page gatherings are separated. Almost all the books in languages other than English are held in the house library: Latin; Greek; French; German; but most interestingly these shelves in the smoking room hold books in te reo Māori, which raise sharp contact-zone questions. Why are the books in Māori treasured? Part of the reason is their value as rare books, but probably more importantly they had family connections—Annie Beetham married Thomas Coldham Williams, son of the missionary Henry Williams and nephew of William Williams, who compiled the first Māori dictionary. An inscribed copy of this book was given to her brothers by Annie. There are also copies of the New Testament in Māori. But I think they were also treasured as markers of place, of a new selfhood, a sign of belonging.

I found myself also becoming deeply attached to this site, with its grand trees and Victorian plumbing, flower-painted china and pipe racks by the back door. Because the Beetham family never threw anything away, being at Brancepeth is to smell and see what remains of the 19th century. Opening the books, with their scent of cheap ink and paper and traces of long-ago pipe smoke, enhanced my sense of experiencing what someone before me experienced, a sense of belonging tied to these books and their lives in this place.

I was also preoccupied with the deeply evocative traces of Māori still visible in this English, baronial, squattocratic space, with its turreted house and grand vistas. There is in fact a pre-European landscape which is intermittently visible and hard to read. The stump of a tree felled by adzes has been preserved, labelled, and protected with a little tin roof. There are, I've been told, remnants of a pre-European settlement down on the river flats which I have never seen but which has recently been visited by local iwi, and the garden contains the remembered but vanished presence of Nuku Tewhatewha, a significant pātaka carved for Wī Tako Ngātata of Te Ātiawa, Ngāti Ruanui and Taranaki iwi. It has a particular connection to the formation of the Kīngitanga and expresses something of the relationships among Māori tribal leader—it formed one of what were called the 'Pillars of the Kingdom' and is the only one to survive. Nuku Tewhatewha, which was given to William Beetham by Wī Tako in 1861, lived in the garden at Brancepeth for 70 years before being returned to Te Ātiawa and housed in the Dowse Museum. Wī Tako's friendship with William Beetham is also imaged in Beetham's commanding portrait of Wī Tako and his fellow chief Te Puni with Dr Featherston (1857–8). Documentary evidence at Brancepeth suggests that Hugh Beetham, William's fourth son who ran the station, and his brothers who were shareholders, also maintained a complex network of friendships and other relationships with Māori, partly enabled by their ability to speak te reo Māori.

Māori have a strong and visible textual presence in the ledgers and the station diary. Some of the Brancepeth land was leased from local Māori hapu and kaumatua such as Piripi Iharaira Aporo were frequent visitors in the early years. Rents paid to Māori landowners are always written in red in the 1890s ledgers. The diary is full of references to individual Māori employees, descriptions of their working days, the composition of the 'Māori board' at shearing time, visits by Māori neighbours, deputations and letters to ask Hugh Beetham (Hui Pitama) to come to Land Court hearings and interpret for them. It is not possible to entirely recreate or interpret these relationships, but their traces are everywhere and reveal Brancepeth as an employment hub, regular supply depot and daily port of call for Māori in the late 19th century.

Recently Ed Beetham found some rotting boxes full of papers in the roofspace of the stables. They were thrown out of the station office in 1908 and are now covered in black mould and rat droppings, lacy with holes eaten in their edges. I could only look at them in the open air, carefully peeling back layers stuck together with damp. Many of these papers are in te reo Māori and bear witness to the business transactions and friendships of the 19th century. Brancepeth is now a place where Māori come very occasionally for specific purposes.

Part of my own digging into place at Brancepeth has been spent literally digging into the records kept in the safe in the homestead, a concrete vault built into the wooden house, to protect precious documents from fire. The ceiling weeps a fine white concrete dust onto a huge and unsorted mix of letters, photographs, passports, wills, maps, land titles and legal documents; chill, lifeless air leaches from the walls and ceiling. It is as if the vast eastern terrain of 1890s Brancepeth, long since disaggregated into separate smaller farms, is reassembled in paper, along with all the hills and valleys, the many criss-crossings of class and gender, people and landscape, bosses and workers, readers and books.

There is very little trace of women, other than members of the Beetham family, in the library books or subscription records, but the site has a number of gendered spaces. The laundry room, the pink formal drawing room, the cosy morning room, the nursery, the homestead kitchen and schoolroom, and a row of poky, hot upstairs bedrooms on the other side of the service door were mainly occupied by women. Their names appear in the records and some of their personalities and circumstances are fleetingly described in the station diary, like Alice Odlin, the 'household Venus', but the site now offers very few traces of their habitation. However, marginalia in the library books and the newspaper articles written by the station clerk display insistent and ineradicable sexism. And here is where the world of text and the place in which that text was generated and consumed offer a contact zone—Victorian fiction is overwhelmingly preoccupied with issues of gender and class.

The Brancepeth library contains a very large number of Victorian romances which are among the most heavily used books in the collection. They contain pressed flowers, marginalia, sketches and cigarette butts, dirty pages, loose covers, unravelling bindings. I didn't think I could fully understand what reading meant to the workers on the farm unless I read the Victorian novels they liked and when I did the synergies between them and life in this place leapt out at me. Rural New Zealand in the 19th century had pronounced gender imbalance. At Brancepeth the ratio of men to women was at least 10:1, which makes the Victorian novel's pursuit of the romantic heroine all the more poignant. The social atomisation of colonial New Zealand (most of the 300 male employees who lived and worked on the farm did not have their families with them) makes the Victorian quest for domestic happiness and security entirely germane to the lives of these lonely and often poverty-stricken men. Class, one of the abiding preoccupations of Victorian fiction, is materialised in the farm layout, with different entrances and buildings, and there were variations in hospitality between the trade workers and professional men—the former ate in the men's whare while the professional men took their meals in the saloon. Casual sexism expressed in marginalia and comments about actual people in the station diary reinforced the double bind which was so common to women of all ages but immortalised in Victorian literature—the angel in the house and her doppelganger, the slattern. House cooks invariably fell into the latter category.

The way money flowed and pooled at Brancepeth (wealth and who has it is, of course, the other great theme of Victorian fiction) is visible in the custom-built buggy, the groom's pale blue suede coat and top hat, the silver and portraits and china, the towering trees and spreading lawn. It is also visible in the dry patches. One of the most frequently visited offsite places for the farm workers was the pub at Taueru. Most went there to 'knock down' their cheques. The farm records note the drunks who lost all their money and then their jobs, and the single family bible left behind by the cowman is redolent of the missing possessions and traces of all those working people. The site's absences are as powerful a story of place as anything that is still there: the vanished bush, cleared for paddocks and felled for buildings, the people who used to knock endlessly on the office door annoying the clerk, horses and dogs and bullocks whose labour and noise filled the lane behind the house, the smoke from pipes, cigarettes and oil lamps so thick in the library it was hard to read or breathe.

The vineyard on the hill at the back of the old woolshed, which produced a great quantity of grapes for the family winemaking business in Masterton, was torn out a long time ago but bottles of 120-year-old wine are still kept in the house cellar. Alcohol was one of the hard class boundaries—claret and hock were served at dinner in the homestead but there was a complete ban on alcohol for the men, and instant dismissal followed if they were caught drinking or distilling. The past also throws its shadow in vanished talk, vocabulary and turns of phrase. It took me ages to work out what a 'naked swagger' was. The station diary displays the education of someone who came from a different position in life than you might expect on a sheep station, frequently using phrases in Latin, Greek, French, German, Italian and Hebrew. It was a useful code—the station clerk always noted money sent to his wife in Motueka (usually five pounds) in Greek, so thieves wouldn't know to rob the mailbag. But his insistent display of his education made me feel what reading meant to some of these displaced men—it was quite literally a lifeline.

Because much of what I began to think about place, and the connections between place and reading, only occurred to me over repeated visits to Brancepeth, I felt compelled to build that subjective knowing into my account of its history; to keep myself, as it were, in place. Carolyn Steedman, reflecting on Derrida's term 'archive fever', sees it as 'part of the desire to find or locate or possess that moment of origin, which, in a deluded way, we think might be some kind of truth'. I agree with her that the search for original archival truth is deluded, but I simultaneously think that without the archival dirt that Brancepeth offered me, the gift of other people's detritus which seemed to bring them into the room,

I would have been unable to glimpse the place where past and present were briefly coeval. Nor could I have imagined how what's inside your head might fit with what's outside it, how romantic fiction might interact with life in a whare 20 miles from town and a hemisphere from home, or how you might leave some faint footprint of crossing the printed page on an evening in July. At some points of recognition, it would be untruthful to remove yourself from the narrative you are trying to make.

Note on Sources:

Antoinette Burton, 'Introduction', from *Archive Stories: Facts, Fictions and the writing of History*, ed. Antoinette Burton (Durham, N.C.: Duke University Press, 2005), 11.

Robert Darnton, 'First Steps Toward a History of Reading', from *The Kiss of Lamourette: Reflections in Cultural History* (New York: W.W. Norton, 1990), 154–187.

Jacques Derrida, *Archive Fever: A Freudian Impression*, (Chicago: University of Chicago Press, 1996).

Stephanie de Montalk, 'Super Bug, Rumour and Truth: On Writing a Memoir/Biography of Count Geoffrey Potocki de Montalk', *Journal of New Zealand Studies*, NS 1, October 2001, 63–76.

Emmanuel Le Roy Ladurie, *Montaillou, Village Occitan*, (Paris: Gallimard, 1975), trans. Barbara Bray, (New York: Vintage Random House, 1979).

Mary Louise Pratt, *Imperial Eyes Travel Writing and Transculturation*, (London: Routledge, 1992).

Anne Salmond, *Between Worlds : Early Exchanges between Māori and Europeans*, 1773–1815. (Auckland, NZ: Viking, 1997).

Carolyn Steedman, *Dust: The Archive and Cultural History*, (New Brunswick: Rutgers University Press, 2002).

William Williams, *Dictionary of the New Zealand Language and a Concise Grammar*, (Paihia, 1844).

Lydia Wevers is the director of the Stout Research Centre for New Zealand Studies at Victoria University of Wellington. She is a specialist in New Zealand and Australian literature, and has also published on travel writing and the history of reading. Her latest book is *Reading on the Farm: Victorian Fiction and the Colonial World* (2010).

Writing Pukeahu: A Year (and More) of Walking in Place

Ingrid Horrocks

I

We began our first writing workshop by going on a walk, taking the institutional grey stairs down the side of the building and out. Even though we all stepped through this windowed well day after day, only one of the students would end up writing about this place between places, built in Wellington Polytechnic days. Once on the ground we paused to talk with the men in orange vests who had been working in the car park for months, and they explained they were replacing the water pipes that ran below the buildings, redirecting and containing streams pushed underground.

Then we were off down Tasman Street, moving in conversational pairs that formed and re-formed, passing the brick wall with convict arrows, the works for the new war memorial park, and then climbing up the steps to the National War Memorial Carillon bell tower raised above the city. The Carillon's sides were fretted with scaffold but when we pushed the Hall of Memories doors experimentally, they opened with a sigh and we were sucked into the quiet beyond. It was the first visit for all of us. I wondered if the place had always been open, with its stone cool that reminded me of churches in Europe. Up the front, forming a kind of altar, was a sculpture of three figures, a woman and two children, flat like Henry Moore figures. Were they dancing?

The students were quieter after that, thoughtful spaces opening up within the group as we walked at a new distance from each other. We entered the old Dominion Museum building, now part of Massey University, and dispersed, each finding a place to wander or sit down in the marble quiet of the Great Hall. I sat, too, disarmed by the students' stillness, as well as by the beauty of the space itself.

One of them wrote about how strange it felt to observe this space, which she associated only with rows of desks and the anxiety of exams. An older student told a younger one about how she used to bring her kids here, and stand beneath the airy skeleton of the whale that once hung above. I remembered approaching the building up the hill with my grandfather in his slacks and hat, me 19, he 75. I couldn't recall if we stopped together at the memorial. On this visit, though, he tried—the only time he tried—to tell me about his war experience and all the jerky young men from his wedding film. Two brothers and a brother-in-law, each named after a relative who had died in World World I, gone within three years, lost as far away as Malta and the Sangro River in Italy, and as close to here as the Cook Strait. Downstairs we looked at the ghostly Laurence Aberhart photos of stuffed birds from the former museum collections, frozen in flight.

Then we walked on, stopping to ask each other questions and to point things out, moving across the landscape and occupying it as passersby. PolyHigh crèche, Wellington High School and the mysterious industrial piping on the peeling wall of the school hall, down through Te Ara Hihiko, the glassy architectural wonder built for the Massey Design School the previous year, and constructed precisely so that we could walk through it. We exited in front of the complex of buildings that formed the campus marae. I led us round behind the first building, wanting the students to notice how the flat, glittering surfaces of Te Ara Hihiko looked when seen from behind the prefab walls of the small wharekai, wanting them to notice the contrast, and to reflect.

At the back of the group a nervous shuffle began and two women started saying, *We shouldn't be here, not in this area*. I noticed the two of them had paused. For a moment I hesitated, my confidence shaken. But then I pushed on. I thought they were being too careful, avoiding the complexity of engaging with the fact the marae was right here, in the centre of the campus. We didn't need to section off this one part of the place as off-limits, I reasoned. I didn't want us to walk on by as though the presence of the marae somehow wasn't relevant to us. I'd been welcomed on before, and we wouldn't go right in, just around the corner so we could see.

Then, there was a Māori woman running towards us, her voice raised, her eyes wide. You can't be here. She struggled to catch her breath. You can't be here, she repeated, you need to move back.

We shuffled quickly out of the space she was signalling, her arms making sweeping gestures. At first I was simply part of the stumbling group, a chill jolting the sweet certainty that had held my body just moments before. I noticed a nod of recognition between this woman and the two students whose protest I realised I had completely misread. They had been hesitant because they knew the place and its tikanga, not, as I had thought, because they wanted to avoid it. I realised that the marae was, in an important sense, their place on the campus. And then I had to move towards the woman, to apologise, to try to explain, but mainly to apologise.

As we both caught our breath and managed to slow down, she introduced herself and said we could be welcome, but not like this.

These exploratory walks, which I continued alone and with my creative nonfiction writing workshop throughout the second half of 2014 and beyond, were part of a research project conceived within the university as a way to develop more complex relationships to the site on which Massey Wellington is located. The project was set up by a group of staff led by human geographer Robin Peace in response to a perceived 'thinness' of place within the 21st-century multi-campus university. But it was also brought into being simply as a way of engaging with this site, as one might engage with any location. It set out to ask how experience in a particular place might be 'thickened' by making connections to that place's contested histories, its topographies, its inhabitations and uses, and its stories.

It really began for me with Robin talking in the staff tearoom about the hill on which the campus is located. *What hill?* I thought, then realised that my biking body knew of the effort it took to cycle from any part of the city to the building where I had an office, and in which I sat at my computer and typed into a placeless world. How could I not have known that about the place I'd been coming to work for more than five years?

Pukeahu, I learned, was the name Ngāi Tara had given to this small hill. The project's commissioned archaeological report drew connections between the different uses to which the land had been put: from hillsides of Māori gardens to army barracks, a gaol and a prison on the city skyline where prisoners from Parihaka had been held, as well as convicts condemned to hard labour and, later, conscientious objectors during World War I; to the schools and crèche still here today. I learnt that, renamed as 'Cook's Mount', the hill was at one point set aside as one of the Tenths, the one tenth of the total land obtained by the Crown from Māori that was set aside for 'native reserves', but was then reappropriated by the government to be used by the military. And I learned that the hill had been lowered 25 metres, having been literally dug away at in two major building and excavation projects in 1848 and 1883. Where we walked would have once been inside the body of the earth.

Over these months, as I walked on with my class, I found I'd become involved in something more complicated than I'd anticipated. Robin and another colleague, Fiona Shearer, gave presentations in which they grappled with how staff and students could develop a greater sense of where we were through engagements with the place, and through explorations of the complex interrelationships between its cultural and physical environment. I was repeatedly struck by how they introduced the project, both beginning with their own stories, making this a central part of their methodology as though, perhaps, they felt this was the only thing that could authorise them as Pākehā scholars to speak. Robin began one talk with a description of a cold winter walk across campus after a meeting and with an intimation of the university as a thin place, a corporatised place. She posed the question that arose from this: What else is this place? In her talk she turned first to the pre-human ecology of the place and to the trees here now, including the pōhutukawa, seemingly native but in fact non-indigenous to this area and so, in some way, empty of meaning. She talked, too, of the ubiquitous pink flaxes, now divorced from their once central use in Māori culture. Only then did she move on to discuss the peoples whose claims have been made and remade on this place, including the claims made by those of us here, now.

The first talk was given under the name, *Puke Ahu: Promoting a Place-based Bicultural Campus Identity*, but immediately the PR-word 'promoting' was an issue, and from the outset I, at least, felt uncomfortable with the centrality of the idea of developing an 'identity'. Robin and Fiona specifically argued, though, that the project should not alleviate anxieties by presenting Pākehā in particular with a comforting narrative of belonging. Instead, it should work to create an unsettled imaginary. How might this thinking develop a productive ambivalence to place? they asked. As a group, we came to feel that there needed to be multiple articulations of the place, made always with an awareness that each one would have gaps and unforeseen silences. We would inevitably miss so much, even as we tried to see the place better. And were we aiming to discover a place or construct it? people asked. I'd undertaken to work with my creative writing students to read about imaginings of place and experiment with ways to write about and in *this* place.

The day after our first class, Dale-Maree Morgan, the Marae Taurima (Marae Manager), who, it turned out, was also involved in the Pukeahu project, wrote me a polite email about our 'chat', which I read out in workshop the following week. She sent me some information about the marae atea, the area we had stumbled into, as the place where tikanga Māori is accorded its ultimate expression, and where the pōwhiri (a number of which I had participated in precisely that location) is traditionally meant to test the intentions of manuhiri (visitors), 'to ensure they came in peace rather than coming to confront, cause trouble or incite conflict'. She also explained that if she hadn't approached and invited us through the gate properly, she wouldn't have been honouring her duty to the kawa (protocol) of Te Āti Awa in this place, nor the implicated mana of the university. In workshop we talked about how we had ended up there, what it was about the architecture or the very fact of a campus marae that had made it feel possible and acceptable to explore. As a group we decided to accept Dale's offer to organise a pōwhiri we could join. She emphasised, too, that Te Kuratini Marae was a teaching marae, a place to make mistakes and learn.

Six weeks later Dale sang out her karanga and we walked onto Te Kuratini—the two women from the class who knew the marae well and whose voices on our first visit I had both heard and not heard, opting to come on as part of our group. Even so, we had no one with the knowledge or skills to answer Dale's call of welcome.

My male students and a visiting contractor entered the wharenui first, something I couldn't help returning to in my thoughts and conversations over the following weeks. Once inside the wharenui the men took the front seats, while I started the second row of chairs with my female students, the backs of the men's heads, despite my best efforts, continuing to occupy my vision. Here my liberalism and my feminism were incommensurate, leaving me struggling with unresolved and unresolvable feelings—even as I tried to simply set these thoughts aside as insignificant to this interaction.

One of my students, a woman who was Māori-Chinese and hadn't been brought up with Māori tikanga, would also return to this image in class. Her half-

Māori, half-Chinese grandmother had massaged her nose when she was a child so she wouldn't look 'too Māori', and for her the question of gender dynamics in the space of the marae was a very real source of confusion, and even of pain. I continue to think, too, about Tina Makereti's comment when she read my first attempt at this essay, that being in front (and being able to speak on the marae) doesn't signify the hierarchy some of us gave it except in Pākehā thought, something Dale had also tried to persuade us of before we were welcomed on, although in different terms. The radical challenge of this thinking, as simple as it appears, and my continued inability to know where I stand in relation to it, seems to me to suggest the extent to which Pākehā thought can struggle in a genuinely Māori space. Of course, even this over-simplifies, as though there are such clear-cut, unitary things as Pākehā or Māori world-views.

Later, over a shared lunch in the wharekai, a converted pre-fab classroom with basic tables and chairs, I asked Dale if she would talk with us about Māori concepts of place, whatever that would mean. What she offered back was a demonstration of different peoples, of associations with very *particular* landscapes. Iwi and hapū. She started her talk with the difference between mana whenua and tangata whenua, and immediately, the imaginary idea of New Zealand 'the nation' was gone. Instead there were regions associated with peoples and histories. Dale is Ngāti Maniapoto/Ngāti Raukawa, with no affiliations to the local iwi, Ngāi Tara, Ngāti Ira, Te Āti Awa/Taranaki Whānui. She told us she is of this country but not mana whenua, of this place. She cannot speak for it.

Behind her hung a Robyn Kahukiwa mural from 1987, painted with students from the Polytechnic days, and now marked where tables and chairs have been pushed up against it in the intervening decades. The mural featured the white feather of Parihaka peaceful resistance at its centre with the two taniwha who formed the landscape here, Whātaitai and Ngake. I know these stories through my children's books, where Whātaitai and Ngake are a new part of my family's story times. Only the evening before, the question came up of what Whataitai's call of Auē means—that call of grief when something is lost. Everything is here in this mural, Dale told the students—language, mana, land.

A year later the wharekai would be dismantled to make room for a new wharenui and the mural would go into indefinite storage.

Dale also talked about her Waikato peoples' creation story that has them coming from the earth. Then there was all this drilling and digging of the land, she said. There were misunderstandings, she went on, moving her hands together repeatedly but so that they never quite met. And then the example: if the Anzac War Memorial in front of the Carillon were pulled up, it would be the same as the ripping up of her places of the dead.

II

Some time that August we received an all-staff email confirming that the museum building would be taken back, at least temporarily, for a centennial Anzac exhibition. The creative director was to be Peter Jackson, as though history, especially war, is an action flick, a dam-busting event with fantastic landscapes and visitor numbers. And with excellent export options. As though the history we needed to remember now was only a hundred years old.

I biked the long way to work that day, cycling down the hill from Melrose to Newtown, then up and down again to the intersection between Taranaki Street and the motorway, with its new carvings into the earth. It was still early, but already the trucks backed and beeped, hard at work on the tunnel to make way for the war memorial park. I walked up to the museum building, metal fretwork framed with gold shining gorgeous in the morning sun, and the Carillon in front newly freed from scaffolding.

I'd known for a long time that there was a Parihaka memorial up there somewhere and I'd come to find it. When I did, I was struck by how small it was, off to the west of the museum facade and deliberately non-classical. It is the opposite of monumental, two uncut stones, one the head of a man, one the body. Human-sized, if slightly exaggerated, like human gods in myths. The placard tells the story of the men brought here from Taranaki after the government invasion in 1881 and imprisoned in the gaol on this site before being taken on to the South Island. Some prisoners died while in custody and were buried here. There's a photo of some of the original 170 prisoners sitting on the deck of a transportation ship wrapped in prison blankets in Wellington harbour. They neither look at the camera, nor away. I turned again to the unpolished stone of the sculpture and saw it was a sitting, shrouded figure—at once prisoner, mourner and petitioner.

By the early months of 2015 the name Pukeahu had been adopted for the Pukeahu National War Memorial Park, which would be officially opened on Anzac Day that year. In a space of months the connotations of the name had morphed and been appropriated in the service of a new, old narrative. The build-up to the centenary saturated the news.

I didn't attend the various ceremonies, but later I went to a talk by someone involved in designing the light show that had played across the facade of the museum building for 10 nights. The whole work was shown on the small screen in the workshop room where I teach, alongside a YouTube clip of how extraordinary it had looked bleeding across the museum's face. The original concept, the designer told us, had been to produce a work that would evoke all the conflicts Aotearoa New Zealand has been involved in. The researchers had become interested in the site itself, Pukeahu, producing in their first vision of the work an evocation of the pā that may have been there, the prisoners who were brought through, and the closeness of waka on water. But those who vetted this original imagining saw its narrative as at once too complicated and too specific. Instead, the public show became a carefully framed story, a narrative of two world wars, beginning with tukutuku panels and exquisite imagery of pīwakawaka, but then shifting to the New Zealand flag, images from 1914 and phrases such as 'to maintain our heritage'. It became an act of nation-making explicitly dependent on a projected thinness of place. A play of lights and a story of a united nation fighting wars abroad. Beneath, the site became a screen that blocked out as much as it showed, rather than becoming what it might have been—a porous, articulate and ultimately disruptive and unsettling particularity of place. But the officially projected image of a group of Māori soldiers sitting on board a ship abroad, guns in hand, must have flashed silently across the faces of the men in the photograph on the Parihaka memorial.

III

In November 2014 I assembled a group of staff and students from Creative Writing and Design to develop an online anthology of writing from and about Pukeahu. It was essentially meant to be a student project, conceived of as something to be worked on by those who had become interested in ideas of place, and then to be used in teaching the following year. But as these things do, it grew. It began from an intuitive sense on my part that interesting as documents such as archaeological reports and architectural histories are, that what was still missing from the archive of the project were stories—human experiences of the place. Bringing together stories of people real or imagined traversing and living in and around Pukeahu, Mt Cook, might call up new populations of both past and present. At once alive and ghostly, the inhabitants of these stories might speak together (and to us) of their lives and thoughts in this place. As poet Lynn Davidson, who came on at this stage to help lead the editorial team, later wrote in the anthology's preface, the dynamic relationship between present and past is something that 'novels, essays, and poems understand, easily or uneasily', and that even when particular histories are 'memorialised so determinedly that the memorial becomes a landmark', these histories still remain fluid and impressionable.

We started with just a few stories: Witi Ihimaera's group of men and women from *The Parihaka Woman* coming to the gaol at Pukeahu to enquire about a relative who has disappeared; Alison Wong's Chung-shun and his younger brother Chung-yung in *As the Earth Turns Silver* heading to Haining Street for wontons and noodles and chatting with a constable in the brick police station on

Tasman Street; and Robin Hyde's John in *The Godwits Fly* giving up his bicycle (and his swearing) when the family moves down the hill from Melrose, and catching 'rheumatism, bibliomania and politics, none of which he could afford'.

The people involved took their own interests out onto the hill and the city around, and brought back different findings: Thomas, the walker, brought histories, accounts of buildings and tram accidents, and his own photographs of street art; Lena brought many things but, most wonderfully, her own written meditation on the place and an excerpt from Katherine Mansfield's gritty, early story 'Ole Underwood', with the 'prison perched like a red bird' above the city; and Rosie, the designer, found photographs and brought her imaginings of how the stories might look and feel if uploaded to the digital world and made navigable from *any* place. Links and connections between texts emerged that surprised us, most notably, perhaps, the (often uneasy) presence of the New Zealand Chinese community here across so very many pieces of writing and across time. After much discussion, we decided to include an essay by Lynn Jenner in which the only link to Pukeahu is a reference to the Holocaust Centre of New Zealand on Webb Street. In the longer piece this comes from, Jenner juxtaposes meditations on refugees from the Holocaust with a visit to a Wellington exhibition of photographs of Syrian refugees. This piece of writing seemed to evoke not just the still-present complexity of who gets to live in which places—including in this place—but also the inevitable presence of multiple places in each of our interior worlds.

On an afternoon in May 2015, Lynn Davidson and I took a printed draft of what was by that point called *Pukeahu: An Exploratory Anthology* to the university café, Tussock. Jacob Tapiata from the office of the assistant vice-chancellor (Māori and Pasifika) was down from the Manawatu campus and had agreed to meet with us. The question I had emailed him was to do with the use of te reo Māori for section headings in the anthology. It was a simple question, I'd thought. In particular, Lynn and I had jointly written a preface which we wanted to act as a kind of welcome to the anthology, a kind of karanga or calling in. We wondered if there was a Māori phrase that we might use to evoke this.

Jacob phoned me and asked why we wanted to use te reo Māori, what that would mean. It would be best if we talked in person. In Tussock, we talked for a long time, and then Jacob started drawing on a napkin, suggesting a possible shape for the anthology as a whole. It could work like a whare whakairo, a meeting house that would encompass and hold the many voices as part of a single story. The section headings themselves could work as a kind of poem, with a metaphorical pattern woven between them. His pen moved rapidly against the fragile paper, building up drawings and words.

I couldn't fully follow what he was saying. What I understood, though, was that if he had been involved from the beginning, the anthology could have been a very different work. As he drew he illustrated a huge loss in potential imagining. It also became apparent, as he in a sense introduced us to the histories and possibilities of telling stories in this place, that of course we weren't entitled to make that call of welcome. Those prefaces should, I have come to think, have been imagined more as a kind of offering to place. If we did this again, we would start rather than end with this conversation.

Jacob also looked at our line-up of section titles and wanted to know why the anthology didn't start from the 'beginning'. He suggested it should reflect the 'real history' of this place, and told us about what the dedication of the new memorial park the previous month meant in terms of the bringing together of Ngāi Tara and Te Āti Awa after centuries of conflict. With this question of 'real history' came implied questions of real politics, real land and conflict, and real issues of historically inscribed economic inequalities. As Alice Te Punga Somerville writes later in this collection, it is not enough to say 'in my view'—there are truths. A shorter version of Alice's essay also formed part of the Pukeahu anthology itself.

In the café we found it hard to articulate why we had structured the anthology the way we had, but the question prompted us to think more about what we were seeking to do in relation to place. The material we had gathered had called for a questioning of narrative history. We, too, had originally imagined a kind of literary timeline mapped onto place—one thing sitting over the next, each adding an additional layer. But where would we place Hyde's 1930s evocation of a moment from the turn of the century or Alison Wong's very different story of the same place at the same moment, but published in 2009? In the absence of having found texts by early Māori writers, would Elsdon Best get to speak first simply because that was the earliest text we had? More importantly, did a linear trajectory from one thing to another reflect or conjure how people engaged with, or experienced, place? Both Lynn and I started out as poets. We were aware that stories of place don't necessarily work in terms of sequential chapters.

After the conversation with Jacob we made changes, in particular shifting the sections we were calling 'Contesting Histories' and 'Confinement' to earlier, leaving the more contemporary 'Living in Pukeahu' pieces for later, in the hope they might sound out differently as part of an accumulation of stories from the same place. But we kept the section 'Contesting Histories' non-chronological, approaching the often dark histories of the location through juxtaposition of different kinds of imaginings, so that Best's account is immediately challenged by Te Āti Awa journalist Rachel Buchanan's contemporary questioning of how we remember (and fail to remember) colonial and pre-colonial history, and is preceded by Bill Manhire's strange, evocative and musical meditation on icons, iconography and how myths are made. At the opening we placed three new pieces of writing, a haka/waiata by Hinemoana Baker that names the mountains, iwi and hapū who occupied Te Aro Pā, and two new personal essays, one by Te Whānau a Kai, Ngāti Porou, Ngāti Kahungunu artist Angela Kilford and one by Lena. We called these 'Embodied Archaeologies—Excavation Songs', positioning them as kinds of walking tours or guides to the place, propelled by an awareness of the presence of different times within our particular present, as experienced by the moving, speaking voices of those who carried them.

I was reluctant to fully embrace the idea of 'real history' in part, I now think, because it doesn't move me enough. On some basic level I don't understand history. I don't think I'm alone in this. I was glad Lynn was with me after the conversation in Tussock to say, but this is our project, our way in. Aware, even as we spoke, of the terrible awkwardness of this claim. It seemed the only way, though, that we could make—offer, advance—anything. Even an anthology, it turned out, was much more a collective personal essay than we had realised, a guided journey through a place put together by many hands and told in many voices. Such a work could only ever be a partial, subjective, possibly transient articulation, with even more gaps and silences than we'd realised as we were making it. We'd made some steps, then, but we needed to keep moving and talking.

Weeks later, when we returned to Tussock with a new draft to meet with Dale and Jacob this time, Dale suggested using only the phrase 'He kupu whakataki' for the preface and no text in te reo Māori for the section headings. The anthology, she suggested, was both a bigger and a smaller project than the bicultural framework that might be suggested by consistent bilingual headings.

What we had brought together, then, was not quite a local history project, which might suggest a fixed, stable location and a chronological account of events that occurred over time. Nor had we set up Pukeahu as a representative microcosm of the wider nation. Rather, through bringing together multiple personal viewpoints in an almost choral work in which voices speak with, against and over one another, the anthology evokes a place made of multiple constellations of activities, meetings and movements, and an understanding of place as something always being reimagined, always in the process of becoming. Place not as memorial, but as something being made and un-made in the telling. Perhaps such work can call up newly resonant sounds from a place and new ways of speaking histories, which might, in turn, make way for new thoughts and questions, and so different ways of acting in place in the present. What emerges from reading through the anthology for me now is an affective set of connections and stories that still surprises and moves me. The final design makes it impossible to see all of the collection at once, so that the reader must open up different sections or sets of text, which drop down deep into the computer or mobile screen as into the earth. Unlike with a printed book or a plaque, it is designed to be malleable enough to allow for the adding of new writings, both newly found and newly written, brought together by different people in another moment.

As if to confirm the inevitable limitations of our own attempt, despite what it does offer, the week after the anthology went live a colleague sent me a copy of J.C. Sturm's poem 'At the Museum on Puke-ahu (He waiata mō ngā taonga)'. This should have been at the heart of the anthology, but we hadn't even come across it. It ends:

> Our shadows on
> The polished floor
> Kept us company
> Like secret allies
> As we moved toward
> The whare whakairo
> Te Hau-ki-Tūranga
> In the great hall
> Where Tāwhirimātea
> Shattered the air
> Around the high dome
> Above us
>
> And all the old taonga
> Moved restlessly
> In their glass-caged sleep
> Dreaming of their prime
> Of release and being
> Taken home—

'Āwhinatia mai
Arohatia rā'—
Sharing with us
The painful truth
Of irretrievable loss.

Note on Sources:

Unless otherwise stated, all citations, including those from Witi Ihimaera, Alison Wong and Robin Hyde, can be found in Ingrid Horrocks, Lynn Davidson, Lena Fransham, Thomas Aitken (eds.), and Rosie Percival, design, *Pukeahu: An Exploratory Anthology*. http://pukeahuanthology.org/. The editors also talked with Pip Adam about their experience of the project in Episode 23 of Adam's podcast *Better Off Read*: https://betterreadnz.wordpress.com/2015/08/22/pukeahu. I am grateful for the resources made available on the Puke Ahu Campus Identity Initiative site: https://www.massey.ac.nz/massey/initiatives/sustainability/research/living-labs/projects/puke-ahu/puke-ahu.cfm; as well as in 'Before a Board of Inquiry: Basin Bridge Proposal Statement of Evidence of Morris Te Whiti Love for the New Zealand Transport Agency (cultural effects)', 25 October 2013 https://www.nzta.govt.nz/assets/projects/basin-bridge-application/docs/evidence-morris-love.PDF; and the draft of an article, 'Puke Ahu: Articulating a Bicultural, Place-based, University Campus Identity', by Robin Peace and Fiona Shearer, developed from their talks. My general understandings of place have been influenced by many people, but in particular by the work of Doreen Massey. Thank you to Philip Steer for sending me J.C. Sturm's poem, which is quoted here from *Te Ao Mārama: Contemporary Māori Writing*, ed. Witi Ihimaera (Auckland: Reed, 1992), 111–112. Most of all, I am grateful to my students and to all those who have generously talked with me about this project with such patience and generosity. Ngā mihi nui.

Ingrid Horrocks is the author of a travel memoir, *Travelling with Augusta: 1835 and 1999* (2003), and two collections of poetry. She did a PhD at Princeton University and now teaches creative nonfiction and English at Massey University, Wellington. She has published articles in various journals and her book, *Women Wanderers and the Writing of Mobility, 1784–1814*, is forthcoming with Cambridge University Press. More recently she has become interested in exploring relationships between mobility and place in a New Zealand context, as well as in bringing critical and creative writing into closer conversation. Recent projects include a pair of essays which take Martin Edmond's work as their springboard and which appeared in *Sport 43* and *Biography: An Interdisciplinary Journal*.

You take place with you as you go on

Māori Writing in Place; Writing in Māori Place

Alice Te Punga Somerville

What does it mean to write in place? What does it mean to write from place, on place, or to place? Can place re-place a writer? How do Māori write in place? Who writes in place of Māori? Who writes on Māori place? What about Māori in space?[1] I start to sound like Dr Seuss . . . but this word 'place' does that: it folds and unfolds dynamically. I want to leave a question hanging around the edges of these pages: if attending something on someone's behalf can be described as going in their place, how do we determine the difference between Māori writing in place, writing in Māori place and writing in place of Māori?

Placing

The Christchurch earthquakes have become a new 'where were you when' event that has produced, if not a new fault line, at least the overlapping of the tectonic plates of before and after. Lloyd Jones refers to the quakes in his introduction to *Griffith Review 43*; it's the starting point of Jolisa Gracewood and Susanna Andrews's collection for *Tell You What 2015*; and it's referred to in the website description of the December 2014 colloquium on the personal essay. As well as placing a marker on our sense of time, however, earthquakes have also produced place—literally, produced land—as well as expelled it in the form of chasms and liquefaction. So much of the place we now know as Wellington was produced through the activity of Rūaumoko, the activity of earthquakes. Much of Wellington hasn't always been place.

'Placing' is a way of talking about recollection—it can be an admission of partial memory. We might say, 'I know who you're talking about but I just can't place her.' In late November 2014, John Key commented that New Zealand was settled peacefully. Talking about New Zealand's colonial history, Key seemed to say: 'Unpeaceful acts? I can't place them.' And yet, these unpeaceful acts placed him. Place him. Give him place. In this settler-colonial context, unpeaceful acts, whether we can place them or not, structure our relationship to place. They produced place. They still do.

Key's comment actually began with the words 'In my view', a phrase that both claims and disclaims anything that follows. We're smugly astounded he could have it so wrong, and yet those of us who are most smug and most astounded tend also to be deeply committed to notions of perspective, relationality and multiplicity. We cry out that he is not telling the truth, substituting 'actual history' with his 'view', and yet in other contexts we find ourselves getting most traction against suffocatingly singular versions of 'actual history' by claiming the important thing is 'view'. I wonder how we think we can get away with having it both ways. Ah—but there is a difference; of course there is. Perspective doesn't cut it when we are thinking about holocaust denial or blind faith in American justice as meted out in Ferguson; there are truths. There are truths, albeit ones on which we all have different 'views'. There is the truth that the 21st century excavations of Te Aro pā, in what is now inner-city Wellington, found cannon balls amongst the pottery and foundations of raupō walls.

Wellington

Because we moved to Auckland when I was five, my childhood time spent in Wellington was mostly during school holidays. For family events and Christmases we would all drive down—Mum, Dad, my sister and me—but just Megan and I would stay with our grandparents during the May and August school holidays. Besides my actual favourite activity of all time, which was going to the swings at Avalon Park in Lower Hutt with Grandad, one of my other favourite activities was catching the train with him to Wellington. I would press my nose up against the window to watch the part of the harbour that was stained red from the abattoir up on the hill. (The pinkish tinge at the far reach of the scarlet water was the second sign we were getting close; the first sign was a thickening of the density of seagulls flapping around.)

Once we got to the city, Grandad would point out the government building with which he'd been associated throughout his work life (and which is now a Faculty of Law), and remind me—as I've overheard all kinds of people remind each other while walking along that stretch of pavement—this was once the largest wooden structure in the southern hemisphere. Inevitably we would make it up Manners Street and along to Taranaki Street, at which point Grandad—not every time, but certainly more than once—informed me that I mustn't forget the name of the street is connected to our family's own history. The streets of Wellington bore our name! I look back now at my innocent child-self who not only believed Grandad when he said what he did about Taranaki Street, but took it one step further and realised that family names were elsewhere in the city too. Right next to the train station, Bunny Street was surely named after his eldest sister Martha Te Punga who, because of her love of raw vegetables as a child in the 1910s and 20s, was always known in the family as 'Bunny'.

In place

Sometimes when I'm home I still catch that train, invariably thinking of Grandad and our many trips alongside the harbour. Beyond the station I pass through Bunny and walk down Taranaki Street, which starts off being parallel to Tory but after a while runs up the valley alongside Tasman Street. I live across the Tasman at the moment, another kind of Māori cliché, enjoying opportunities in Australia that home hasn't provided: a career, visa and financial situation that works for my small multi-citizenshipped family. One of my recent publications—one that aptly became public not long after I moved to Sydney in mid-2014—is a journal article called 'Living on New Zealand Street: Māori presence in Parramatta', which explores Māori history from the starting point of a Sydney road with a peculiarly cross-Tasman name. Although Tasman Street is in Wellington, New Zealand Street is in Parramatta, now a mere sub-city in the sprawl of Sydney, known to Māori as Poihākena. Yes, there's a New Zealand Street in Poihākena, which is really in Parramatta, but more really Parramatta is the Dharug place known as Burramatta, which means the gathering place of eels. (Parramatta is like Petone: it sounds like an Indigenous word if you don't know the local language, but is the victim of too rough an orthographic move and has departed too far from the prior name to be considered the same. It's also said to be the source of the name Paremata, a suburb of Porirua, northwest of Wellington.) In the article I explain the reason for New Zealand Street in Parramatta (it's one site of Marsden's seminary for New Zealanders back in the early days of the New South Wales colony) and further explain that at the time (the first decades of the 19th century) 'New Zealander' meant Māori.

For me, tracing the personal essay in New Zealand involves the tracing of personal essays written by New Zealanders in this early 19th-century sense. The first piece of published Māori writing was by Mowhee (Tommy Drummond), a young northerner who learned to read and write on Norfolk Island, where he'd gone as a child to live with the Drummond family. He later moved with the family to New South Wales, found farm work to be too boring, and eventually moved in with Marsden in his home; the precursor of the seminary which later was sited on the stretch of land now known as New Zealand Street. Mowhee ended up in London in 1816, and after six months he died and was buried there, but not before he wrote a memoir—*Memoir of Mowhee*—about his experiences.[2] The reverend who hosted him, the Church Missionary Society's Basil Woodd, encouraged him to write about his life, and after Mowhee's passing had it published in several locations as a missionary tract. In the version in *The Christian Journal* 1817, Woodd explains how he has compiled this manuscript:

> Just before we got out of the coach, I said 'Mowhee, you can now write a tolerably good hand. I wish you would, at your leisure, write down what particulars you can recollect of your history. I will keep it, to remember you, after you have departed for New Zealand.' Accordingly, in the course of the week, he undertook this narrative; and had proceeded in it as far as his return to his native islands, at the close of 1814, when his unexpected death prevented farther progress. From this narrative, and from occasional conversation, I have collected the following interesting facts; and so far as I am able I shall insert the statement in his own plain and unaffected words.[3]

We could cry, 'But what of the published version is Mowhee's and what is Basil's?' Some people have cried exactly this, being committed to the idea of an uncontaminated native text which, it seems to me, only means we don't get to claim—don't get to notice, cannot place—Mowhee and a large number of other Māori writers. (And it feels like a selective notion of contamination; after all, whose published writing does not bear the marks of others' editing and revision?) Mowhee's memoir naturalises important things—that Māori write, and Māori travel and Māori write in English, for example—but it also denaturalises other things, such as the stereotypes that become self-important yet unsupportable ideas: that Indigenous people are too wired for collectivity to work in individual (personal) literary forms. Some people claim this about autobiography (despite Mowhee, Kohere and Edwards and all the rest),[4] and perhaps they'll claim it about the personal essay too.

Mowhee is not the only Māori who has written out of place, out of Aotearoa, in another place. Like Abenaki scholar Lisa Brooks, I have sought what I am calling Māori ghost writing despite, or perhaps because of, narratives that render such writing impossible to find. Reflecting on her work on early Indigenous writing in the northeast United States, Lisa recalls:

> When I first began, I was told that looking for writing by Indians would be like looking for needles in a haystack. But I figured if you knew the names of the needles and the places they are from, it might be easier to find them.[5]

Brooks reminds us that finding this writing is not just about locating people ('the names of the needles') but also about identifying place ('the places they are from'). For me, I became as interested in the places they ended up as the places they were from, but the centrality of place is the same. Once I started looking outside as well as inside New Zealand (20 per cent of the Māori community lives outside New Zealand, after all), I found the contours of our writing (and the stories we tell about what it is to be Māori) shifted further still. It's ironic, and yet not, that Māori writing and Māori writing about place extend beyond places that are understood as Māori. Māori and our writing extend beyond whenua Māori but also, to use the familiar (familial) pun, our extension is never beyond whenua Māori. While the priority for a lot of non-Māori scholars and writers is thinking about how they connect to Aotearoa, the story of Māori writing is global. Me? Outside of my own place, I've written on Cayuga, Kanaka Maoli, Mohawk, Anishinaabeg, Dharug and Ngāti Whātua place.

Displace

Wellington wasn't really produced by Rūaumoko. Wellington is produced by us, every time we say it: Wellington. Every time we call its name we re-place, dis-place or perhaps inadvertently mis-place Te Whanganui-a-Tara. And, more specifically, Te Aro Pā, the Taranaki iwi place which was re-placed and then, through the work of certain kinds of history, mis-placed. My Taranaki iwi cousin Rachel Buchanan writes about this place in her book *The Parihaka Album: Lest We Forget* and in articles like 'Why Gandhi doesn't belong at Wellington Railway Station'.[6] Māori stories of Wellington aren't necessarily the same as stories of Māori Wellington. Or, as J.C. Sturm put it in 1955, there's a difference between Māori in Wellington and Māori who 'really belong to Wellington in the Māori sense of the word'.[7] It has become a cliché, Indigenous people calling out contradictory settler nations that proclaim 'Lest we forget' and then refuse to remember. Often the people connected to Te Aro Pā (and Pipitea, Kumutoto, Waiwhetū and all the rest) are invisible. Likewise all of the iwi and hapū who were here before us. No, they're (we're) not invisible. They're (we're) *made* invisible. People assume we exist—logically there must be people local to here—but just can't place us. Even though they're in our place. Living, sleeping, working, loving, eating, thinking, playing, writing in our place. Sometimes, it seems, writing in our place.

We know that Key's 'view' about peaceful settlement is held by many. We would become exhausted if we were concerned with every instance of the holding of that view; our concern in Key's case is his relation to power. But power is not only found in Beehives. Within the New Zealand literary community, when one looks at official events, anthologies and course syllabi, there is little place for Māori; there are few Māori places. This, too, is power: the appearance of collection after collection of writing by Pākehā New Zealanders, whatever the genre, with one or two dollops of brown. To pick one from a lineup of possible examples, of the 63 poems in the 2011 anthology *Best of Best NZ Poems* only four are by Māori authors.[8] Diasporically restricted from bookshops that sell such volumes, I asked my sister in Wellington to buy a copy and send it to me. She called me after taking it home and checked that I still wanted it; she'd read the contents page and saw what I had feared. She offered to take it back to the bookshop. 'Maybe I'll say they should give my money back,' she joked, 'because the claim on the cover is false advertising.' In 2015, at least according to a Google search of courses and prescribed texts—which is an inexact method to be sure—English departments in New Zealand universities taught six books by four Māori writers. (Including drama, eight books by six Māori writers.) The books on offer imply that nobody Māori has published anything worth reading (or at least teaching) since 2005 or written fiction since 1994. There are no courses in Māori literature outside Māori Studies courses that focus on Māori language texts. The method may be woefully inexact, and surely there are exceptions and defensive arguments to be made, but the fact remains that there seems to be little room for Māori in New Zealand literary place.

Perhaps stupidly, perhaps blindly, perhaps naively, I still live in hope that New Zealand will start to collect differently, to curate different conversations, to teach differently, to produce not just writing about place but writing that speaks from and to and with place. I'm not talking about a quota system (although I believe in those and, heck, it might be a good place to start); I'm talking about a willingness to critique power as it can be manifest in New Zealand literary circles at multiple levels. For Aboriginal scholar and writer Tony Birch, when Indigenous people ask the question 'Whose place is this?' the question is not merely 'Who has been here?' in a layered, chronological or tectonic sense, but rather 'Who have we hosted?' In his essay 'The last refuge of the "Un-Australian"', he writes:

> Our legitimacy does not lie within the legal system and is not dependent on state recognition. It lies within ourselves . . . We need to claim our rights, beyond being stuck in an argument about the dominant culture's view of land rights or identity. [See? view!] And we need to claim and legitimate our authority by speaking out for, and protecting the rights of others, who live in, or visit our country.[9]

I can, and I will, complain and write and teach about the persistent enforced narrowness in the official world of New Zealand letters, but Birch reminds us that we can also be the host: the collector, the anthologist, the curator, the MC. The story of New Zealand writing is our story to tell too; where do we start when we tell it? Our story might go all over the place. It might spend time in Taranaki Street in Wellington, New Zealand Street in Burramatta and maybe even Haining Street too.

Eels

There's a link between Burramatta and Te Aro Pā: they are both gathering places of eels. In a publication connected to his doctoral research into the teaching of New Zealand history at high school level (something a few of us probably agree might have come in handy for Mr Key), Richard Manning writes about the work he did bringing together high school history teachers and Māori local iwi representatives in Wellington to talk about the difference between local, Māori and New Zealand histories. Manning describes the visit they take to Waitangi Park, the area down by Te Papa, and the way in which the former Waitangi lagoon was mightily disrupted by two events: the major 1855 Wellington earthquake, and the laying of pipes during the 19th- and 20th-century projects of public works which means the Waitangi stream now exists almost entirely underground through pipes. He cites a Te Ātiawa interviewee who relates: 'People were also quite surprised to find that though there's no stream, because it's all in an underground pipe now, there's still a large quantity of eels living in the Waitangi stream.'[10]

Wellington is a place under which eels are gathering, migrating, continuing to move. The Waitangi stream still runs beneath this place, and when I say this I can't help but recall an elder of mine who came to visit me in my office when I started a job in English at Victoria University of Wellington. She pointed out to the street, which lay there heavy and grey, nine floors down from my office, and said, 'That's the Kumutoto stream—whenever you're here remember this is Kumutoto and it runs down the hill and out to the harbour.' Manning's interviewee goes on to say: 'They hadn't learned the history of that stream or that the stream's now in a pipe.'[11] Manning assumes the interviewee is referring to the people who hadn't learned these things, but it seems to me this could equally mean the eels. No one told the eels their stream was now a pipe, or, we might say, the eels still inhabit their stream. Which is to say, we still inhabit our stream. And for eels—for us—any particular stream in Aotearoa cannot help but flow to an entire ocean and other shores.

Notes on Sources

1   This phrase references the 1975 text that is arguably the first novel composed in the Māori language; it involves space travel. Mataira, Kāterina Te Heikōkō. *Te Atea*. (Wellington: School Publications Branch, Department of Education, 1975).

2   Mowhee, 'Memoir of Mowhee', *Missionary Papers* (London: Church Missionary Society, 1818).

3   Basil Woodd, 'Memoir of Mowhee, a Youth from New-Zealand, who died at Paddington, Dec 28, 1816', *Christian Journal, and Literary Register* 1.23 (13 December 1817).

4   Rewiti Kohere, *The Autobiography of a Maori* (Wellington: Maori Purposes Fund Board, 1951). Mihi Edwards wrote three autobiographies, beginning in 1990. Mihipeka Edwards, *Mihipeka: Early Years* (Auckland: Penguin, 1990). Judith Binney, working with a manuscript connected to the Salvation Army, describes Maraea Morete as the first Māori woman to write an autobiography. Judith Binney, *Stories Without End* (Wellington: Bridget Williams Books, 2010), 315.

5   Lisa Brooks, *The Common Pot: The Recovery of Native Space in the Northeast* (Minneapolis: University of Minnesota Press, 2008), xxxv.

6   Rachel Buchanan, *The Parihaka Album: Lest We Forget* (Wellington: Huia, 2010); Rachel Buchanan, 'Why Gandhi Doesn't Belong at Wellington Railway Station', *Journal of Social History* 44 (2011).

7   J.C. Sturm, 'The Ngatiponeke Young Maori Club', *Te Ao Hou*, 12, 1955, 59.

8   Bill Manhire and Damien Wilkins, *Best of Best New Zealand Poems* (Wellington: Victoria University Press, 2011).

9   Tony Birch, 'The Last Refuge of the "Un-Australian"', *UTS Review* 7.1 (2001) 20.

10 Richard Manning, 'A Critical Pedagogy of Place? Te Ātiawa (Māori) and Pākehā (Non-Māori) History Teachers' Perspectives on the Teaching of Local Māori and New Zealand Histories', *Indigenous Education* 4 (2011) 5.

11 Manning, 5.

Alice Te Punga Somerville (Te Ātiawa) is a scholar, poet and irridentist who lives with her husband in Sydney. Because she is an academic, most of her writing is scholarly (her first book was *Once Were Pacific: Māori Connections to Oceania* [University of Minnesota Press, 2012]); she also writes the occasional poem. Alice is presently teaching Indigenous Studies at Macquarie University (Sydney), and holds a tenured position as Associate Professor of Pacific Literatures at the University of Hawai'i-Mānoa.

Childhood Haunts

Annabel Cooper

Places, says Nigel Thrift, are 'passings which haunt us'. You imbue them with meanings and stories but they embed themselves in you, too. You take shape in and through their topographies, their climates, their light, their buildings, plants and spaces, the presence of people who occupy them with you, the traces of people there before you. You move, places change, but they leave their imprints. Even in an increasingly transient world, you take place with you as you go on.

Writing about the southern Dunedin suburbs—'the Flat'—with the geographer Robin Law around fifteen years ago made me notice how place can be so much more formative than you might anticipate. It seems particularly true of place that 'we know more than we can tell'.[1] There is a quality in the complexities and layers of places that is to a large degree indefinable, but which being there brings upon you, or plants perhaps secretly within you. 'The places in which we live, live in us', says Dylan Trigg.[2] To approach this elusive but important element, I think you need both the kinds of evidence that the social sciences deal in, and an approach that tries to grasp that elusiveness in a more affective way, coming sideways at the difficulty of pinning down something that is at the same time far too familiar and far too hard to describe.

Thrift tackles the difficulty of apprehending place in his essay 'Steps to an Ecology of Place'. He objects to what he calls 'the building perspective' in geography, that is, the idea that 'space and time are neutral grids . . . over which and in which meaning is "placed"'. This, he argues, is a reductively textualist or representational view.[3] Places are dynamic and so complex that, says Thrift, we should accept that we can't entirely know them; and besides, we are always so much *in* them, and we trail them so much with us, that it would be self-defeating to imagine we can fully see or describe them. Yet work with place we must because, he argues, places are so intimately entangled with the memories that form and inform us.

His is a British geographer's view but it holds some possibilities for thinking about Aotearoa New Zealand, where tangata whenua and later settlers have varying kinds of connectedness to places. In this essay I think back over some of my own past work. Some of it has addressed place and the ways we think about it directly, some more obliquely. Each of these studies is about distinctive individuals and their memories of the circumstances which shaped them—in each case, place has resonated strongly in these shaping forces. The narratives of childhood here are stories of a settler-colonial society, forming itself in place and in the context of the shifting meanings of place. Even within the same periods, or the same places, these individuals' recollected encounters with New Zealand places are very different from each other: Mary Isabella Lee, a transient colonial child looking for safe harbour in the South; James Cowan, child of a settler-soldier family in the Waipa Valley; Keith Sinclair, growing up happy and confident by a 20th-century Auckland beach; and Peter Wells, same beach, different boyhood.[4] To reflect now on the paths that led me to research first one of these people-in-place and then another is, suddenly, to be aware of place going to work in me, too; to recognise that where I knew it was some*thing* about these people that brought them to my attention, it was at least in part the *place* about them. Each of them was shaped in, and formed by, places which had already situated themselves in me, a beach-suburb Aucklander with family roots in the Waikato, who has lived for a long time in Dunedin, reshaped by its spaces and climate but still drawn by the pull and feel of the North Island. My own absorption in these lives, one after another, is in itself a little story about the formative character of place.

Southland and Otago: Mary Lee

In her old age, living in Wellington, Mary Lee wrote about coming to Otago and Southland as a child from Scotland. Hardly models of upwardly mobile pioneers in search of prosperity, Lee's parents both had violent tempers and her mother drank heavily. They fought with their families in Scotland and 'desided, That they might be Better away from Relations [*sic*]', but a journey round the world simply relocated the fighting.[5] From their arrival in 1877 they fought and drank their way from Dunedin to Invercargill and many little towns in between, leaving the marks of a transient childhood on their daughter, both literally and affectively. In the first three years in the colony, they moved 11 times, touching down in Dunedin, Oamaru, Enfield, Waimate, Timaru, Geraldine, Timaru, St Andrews, Timaru yet again, Washdyke and back to Oamaru. In Oamaru, just before she turned ten, Lee's mother threw a mug at her, resulting in a head wound, a hearing impairment that became total deafness in adulthood, and periodic blindness. As the drinking and violence got worse, the family moved more to escape the notice of missioners and teachers.

When Mary Lee married things were little better: the settled home with 'nise things' that she had hoped for lasted three weeks before the owner's family reoccupied it and the Lees had to decamp to a one-roomed whare. Soon after this she went to Dunedin to have her first baby, and on her return found her husband had moved again, to the site of a leased surface coalpit in the Waikaka Valley. While Alfredo Lee headed away for temporary farm work and treated the pub on his wages, Mary was stranded out in the country with a newborn baby, only the food that could be grown or caught on the property, and drinking water contaminated with typhoid.

Lee arrived young at the conviction that it was much better to be in some places than others. In the year they were in Invercargill, when she was 12, her mother sent her to work and she 'never was at School, it was a very unhappy year'. The following year she replied to an ad placed by one of her father's former employers, and got him a job back in the little Southland township of Woodlands, where she was able to go back for two more years of school. She was a favourite pupil, she went to picnics and dances, and the teacher ran a library which kept her supplied with books. She read secretly at night and—giving us an unexpectedly evocative little cameo of a rural childhood—sitting by the road. She recalls how, when she was taking the younger children out in the pram, and was far enough away from the house to be out of her mother's sight

> I would sit down By the road Side & read—Sometimes my Sister would tell Mother that I had been reading Instead of Wheeling them about & I would get a Wallaping . . . In 1 year I had read every Book worth Reading & then while I was quite quite happy we moved on to Mataura.

Tony Ballantyne's recent research on the print culture of Gore, another Southland town, helps us to interpret the value Lee placed on reading and her access to the small local library started by the schoolteacher. Gore and its environs, Ballantyne shows, had a vibrant literary and reading culture that not only informed its citizens about the wider world, but underpinned their social and community lives: 'the centrality of print culture and mutual improvement societies . . .

shaped community formation'.[6] For Lee, school, its library and its social activities provided a community beyond the family, a vital source of protection as well as pleasure and knowledge. Lee's pursuit of books was at the same time a pursuit of independence, and she recognised that Woodlands provided the resources.

In Mataura the town's religious life provided community outside family and distinct pleasures that later evoked in her strong memories of a life in place:

> Dureing this Time a Church of Christ, Revival Mission, Started, The Missioner Mr Floyd, came from America. One night when I was with the Army people marching over Mataura Bridge, and Singing—we halted on the Bridge & Looked over—& on the River Bank the Mission People were holding a Meeting & a Baptisam, & as it was a glorious moonlight night, it was worth remembering—the Salvation Army hurried across the Bridge & Down on the Riverbank & Joined the Others in Their Meeting & Singing—altogather it was a happy time.

Hurtled around the southern provinces as a child and a young woman, she staked out her autonomy through location. In Dunedin she found the family a new house so she and her younger sister could have their own room, because 'i was Beginning to have a Bit of Respect for myself'. Not long after, following another outburst of maternal violence, Lee put a bundle of her things out the bedroom window and departed. There is a sense of triumphant finality as she ends this account: 'But i was gone & I never properly went home to my Mothers house for 10 years'. Some years later, leaving her husband after he aims a drunken blow at her and hits the baby instead, she thinks once more of strategic relocation: 'somehow it Just came to me then that I could not Live there any Longer—I would get the Children & myself to Dunedin where I could get work, to get food'. In Dunedin she stayed longer and longer in the houses she rented, charting out her social standing in terms of security of tenure.

Lee grew up buffeted by the repeated loss of community and protection that stability provided in the colonial world of southern New Zealand. Her life made it particularly apparent—and she understood this well herself—that to the extent that places are constituted by their social fabric, some places protect, support and enable one to make one's own way. Other places, because of remoteness, the lack of such essentials as food and clean water, the lack of friends, or the presence of others who fight and drink, present dangers. In the absence of much agency over these forces in situ, Lee fought to make decisions about where she would live.

North Dunedin became the place where she put down roots and made a life. Most of the homes she found during her adult life were within sight of the university campus. They were within walking distance as I edited her autobiography in the early 1990s, though they were no longer standing. It seemed important, as far as possible, to trace her paths around the lower South Island, to see what those places looked and felt like, and imagine what they might have been like then. It was an odd experience and I was never sure how much place could communicate across time. Standing in a paddock in the Waikaka Valley and looking at the prosperity brought by generations of sheep and careful farming in between her moment there and mine, it was hard, except for the cold and the low cloud, to imagine a little one-woman coalmine, a box to put the baby in while she worked, and no running water. In North Dunedin much of the built fabric of her time persisted, though the student dwellers occupied their larger, more comfortable houses with much less pride than Lee when she had staked out her ground in tiny leg-in cottages a century earlier.

Ōrākau and the Waipa Valley: James Cowan

Lee's Southland was the home of Ngāi Tahu and an already densely intermarried population, but hers is a settler story in which Māori are mentioned only once, riding into town to help put out a fire in the night. Where James Cowan grew up, at Ōrākau in the Waipa Valley, the Māori past of place was inescapable.

Cowan's work speaks in a very different way about what place can make of us. Nearly everyone who has written about him points out the locality of his childhood, although not everyone has noted the distinctiveness of his reflections on it. He grew up, son of a settler-soldier, on confiscated land on the site of the Battle of Ōrākau, arriving there in 1870 as an infant only six years after its former occupants had been compelled to leave it. The farm was on the border of the Rohe Pōtae, then still controlled by the Kīngitanga.[7] From a childhood fascination with the already-fabled past of the area, Cowan went on to produce an immense corpus of journalism, short nonfiction and history about the Māori past, including a remarkable official history of the New Zealand Wars, which derives from extensive oral histories from all sides of the conflicts.[8] His interviews with Māori veterans constitute a valuable and highly unusual collection of records of colonial conflict.

About the same time as he wrote the official history, Cowan wrote a local history of the Waipa. He introduces his own upbringing there by describing the view from the farm where he grew up in the decades after the Waikato War:

> Looking southward across the Puniu in the Seventies and early Eighties we who were bred up on the Frontier saw a mysterious-appearing land, fascinating to the imagination because unknown—a land, too, of dread in the years of unrest, for there in the hinterland only a few miles from the border river lived Te Kooti and his band and the hundreds of Waikato dispossessed of their good lands on which we Pakeha families now dwelt.[9]

Cowan grew up knowing very well how he got to live in the place that provided this view—a place beloved by him, but also by the people who no longer lived there. Through much of Cowan's childhood King Tāwhiao and his exiled Waikato people lived on the southern side of the Pūniu, 'looking down with many mournings on the good lost lands and the lost battlefields of the Sixties', returning only after the peace-making to 'their old ancestral homes, or what was

113

left of those homes, on the west side of the Lower Waikato'.

Cowan was a child of this landscape like no other. He was familiar with blockhouse construction and frontier defence strategies, as all settlers were in the decades after the war. He tells stories of special hiding places and escape routes, and the periodic scares and alerts. At the same time, he was acquiring his fluency in te reo Māori and seeking out the Māori veterans of Ōrākau, laying the foundation for his formidable knowledge of the wars, and his capacity to write from conflicting points of view.

Many soldier records mention the peaches that grew in the Waikato in the mid-19th century, killed off later by an invading blight. There is a symbolic dimension in these stories about the fighting that took place in peach groves, as if they mark out the wars as a fall from a pre-war paradise. Undoubtedly conscious of this motif by the time he was writing in the early 1920s, Cowan writes about the peaches and the peach trees in the Waipa, listing the names of the places where they grew—names already more famous as sites of the Waikato War. Cowan's evocation weaves between three points in time: the Māori planting of the trees before the war, the abundance inherited by the soldier-settlers, and the moment of writing in the 1920s, which looks back to a plenitude associated with place that can't be retrieved any more. This is an inherently nostalgic reminiscence:

> ... and, above all, the peaches ... peaches vanished, a kind never to be tasted by the present generation. Orakau, Kihikihi, Te Awamutu, and Rangiaowhia were then the favoured land of the most delicious fruit that ever this countryside has known. Peach-groves everywhere, the good Maori groves, trees laden with the big honey peaches that the natives called korako because of their whiteness. Tons of peaches grew in those groves, and those wanted were gathered by the simple process of driving a cart underneath and sending one of us youngsters up to shake the branches until the cart was filled with fruit.

This apparent seamlessness between the (Māori) planting and the (settler) harvest is picked apart as the inquiring child discovers the trees' other legacy. The variety of peaches was in reality lost through blight, but here Cowan implies it was a casualty of war:

> . . . it was curious, too, to explore some of these old groves of trees, on the crown of the farm near the road, for there the lead flew most thickly in the three days' siege of Orakau, and nearly every tree bore the curious weals and knotty growths that indicated a bullet-wound, and a search with a knife sometimes revealed a half-flattened ball or fragment of one.

In a trajectory opposite to that of Lee, Cowan began life as a settler but ended up a traveller, spending a fair amount of his career tracing the past of central North Island landscapes, traversing the sites of the New Zealand Wars and talking to veterans from both sides, but writing about the Māori past of North Island places on a much broader scale too. He liked to travel on horseback best—close to the landscape, and slowly, rather than rushing by in a car. He preferred to travel with people who knew the past of the landscape well, and most commonly travelled with tangata whenua. Even while Cowan celebrated the work of 'missionaries, soldiers, surveyors, road-builders' as well as farmers, he persistently stitched whenua back into place, working to extend Pākehā public memory of place back beyond European occupation.

Cowan seems to me to be a significant figure in thinking about Pākehā conceptions of place, for two related reasons. First, because of this persistent effort to keep alive the Māori past of place. And second, because I suspect that one way or another he had a degree of success. Either he did what he did well, or these views can't have been entirely radical, because for several decades Cowan was the country's most widely published and widely read writer on the subjects of travel, place and Māori, across several media and in a number of genres. Aside from his books of various kinds, his writing was syndicated in a number of newspapers, he wrote a regular feature for the *Railways Magazine*, which was very widely circulated, and his stories kept appearing in the *School Journal* for decades after he died. So, despite the current postcolonial critique which emphasises the forgetting associated with indigenous dispossession, if we are going to understand the shaping of Pākehā sensibilities about place in the first half of the 20th century, Cowan's is still a body of work we must take into account.

Disadvantage or privilege, violent or nurturing families, transience or settlement, South or North Islands, mark out some of the striking distinctions between the childhood recollections of Mary Lee and James Cowan. Colonial places carried meaning for them in such different ways: they had encountered different environments and different communities, a tenuous hold on places setting out the starting point of each life but in strikingly different ways. They each wrote about other violent and unsettling sides of the dream of settlement: in Mary Lee's writing, the violence was located inside the settler family; in James Cowan's, violence sat just beneath settlement itself, beneath the family's very presence in the landscape.

Point Chevalier: Keith Sinclair and Peter Wells

Keith Sinclair's and Peter Wells's autobiographies are located in a newer, more modern and urban landscape—the suburb—a generation or so apart (the 1930s, and the 1950s–60s respectively). It's the same suburb, Point Chevalier in Auckland, but very different. Both of them grew up in a place situated at a point of tension in a national imaginary, as Pākehā New Zealand urbanised. Was New Zealand the land of the outdoor childhood lived in open country, or of built-up urban space, the territory of thousands of private households? In Point Chevalier, the beach was just along the road, the sections large and a bit wild, when the Sinclairs arrived in 1931. By the 50s and 60s when the Wells family lived there, the spaces were closing up as more houses were built. When

I read their two autobiographies, I was struck but not surprised by the radical contrasts in the ways they remembered place.

Though both men would grow up to acknowledge and explore indigenous pasts, their childhoods were lived in mostly Pākehā worlds. Sinclair's and Wells's memoirs of boyhoods both mine a national narrative that formed, already perhaps nostalgic, some time in the early 20th century and found perfect expression in the Point Chevalier of the early to mid-20th century: the free childhood located on the coast, the beach, the reef, in the open spaces beyond the houses—minimally governed by adults who only expected to coincide with children to feed them and see them off to bed. This is an apparently innocent place which we seem to long to have back again, a persistent form of national nostalgia.

It's an imagined place, in a sense, but it is not, in Thrift's terms, a fiction overlaid on a neutral space. And to understand that you still need, I think, the kind of evidence the social sciences yield. Keith Sinclair was pre-eminent among the first generation of historians to focus on New Zealand history. His last major historical study, *A Destiny Apart* (1986), charts the conscious articulation of an emerging national identity, and was written only a few years before he turned to write his autobiography. When he writes about his own childhood, locating his life so precisely in the title—*Halfway Round the Harbour*—Sinclair notes the specificities of place. In Point Chevalier the material and social conditions included the growth of low-density suburbs in the interwar period; Auckland's demography through the early and mid-20th century; the mix of owner-occupied and rental housing; the peninsular topography of Point Chevalier, which like many New Zealand suburbs was close enough to wildish spaces. The scaled-down Californian bungalows like the Sinclairs' gestured towards lives more oriented to the outside. The large sections, the proximity of the creek, the mangrove flats, the wondrous reef and beach, were all material realities feeding a national imaginary.

Although Sinclair and Wells both wrote their Point Chev pasts within this shared cultural memory, shaped by a common material world, they wrote themselves into it from very different perspectives. Keith enters the narrative with abundant delight, recalling how an egalitarian community of kids ranges off over the reefs and around the watery edges of the little harbour peninsula, catching fish and making boats that they could paddle up Meola Creek, scarcely stepping inside between breakfast and bedtime. In Sinclair's memory there is no richer place for a childhood, no more fertile an environment for nurturing body and imagination, and his enthusiasm is deeply persuasive. The world at the back door is varied and welcoming; eldest of a wharfie's ten children, he understands material deprivation but also that he has inherited the rich privileges of the less quantifiable elements of place.[10]

Peter Wells is equally conscious of the national narrative of the outdoor childhood and the privilege it is understood to bestow; but in his *Long Loop Home: A Memoir* his childhood story slaps it in the face. The free and easy space is a paradise denied him by an alienating mix of sexuality and class: Peter and his brother, growing up gay, live at odds with that imagined world. Despite the egalitarian rhetoric attached to the story of the free childhood, it was after all a place of alienation and exclusion for them. There is nothing more damning for Peter to say, in the face of the national story, than: I went inside. The pleasures and the bodily ease of the young Sinclairs become exposure and vulnerability for the Wells.[11] So the contrast between these personal stories drew attention to how sharply personal and cultural memories can diverge and how strongly place can mark out these differences. But Wells's experience may also mark the way in which the unmanaged, unsurveilled openness of the surburb was disappearing, evaporating even between the 1930s and the 1950s as more houses were built, filling in the empty sections and creating a more disciplined suburban landscape. The spaces where kids could once happily disappear for hours on end became rather more known, more visible, more public, and the wild child's world retreated into the past.

Wells fled to Sydney, leaving a place he experienced as both constraining and threatening, for a more anonymously urban place that was defining itself as a gay city. It wasn't entirely a matter of sexuality. A few years later, the young and heterosexual Jane Campion headed across the Tasman, also looking to escape a culture she experienced as confining, introverted and repressed, seeing in Australia a more open, informal world. She has been back and forth since, but her vision of New Zealand (from *An Angel at my Table*, to *The Piano*, to *Top of the Lake*) maintains that dark, ominous tone of subterranean forces working beneath the scenic splendour. Wells, I think, would find this vision entirely familiar.

Conclusions

In all these lives, places were 'passings that haunted', leaving their imprints in the adults who were once children there. What I take from this now is the idea that, although places are in so many ways impermanent, always in the process of becoming something else, what they were at a certain point nevertheless continues to anchor how you go on to become. This operates mostly like a haunting, glimpsed in your peripheral vision, something embedded in personal and in cultural memory that you can never entirely delineate. You know more than you can tell. Prosaically, in a social scientific way, this has to do with material conditions, the landscapes and social circumstances that seep into you in ways that you usually don't, as an individual, map out, or not until later, and only incompletely. So the academic disciplines that deal in such things have much to tell us about who we are as creatures in and of place. Yet the effort to grasp place also eludes strictly academic writing and demands something more particular and personal. As well as the material and social, there are much more ineffable and emotional elements that do matter in the course of individual lives in place—how a library, or a walk with the Salvation Army across a bridge in Mataura at night might tie a child to protective communities; how the remembered taste of peaches can stand for a history of dispossession; how 'outdoors' can be magic for one boy and full of fears for another. All these writers reflect on themselves in place in the medium of memoir or autobiography, genres often thought of as peripheral, unreliable sources. Yet such forms, I hope to have shown here, open a door to the more elusive dimensions of place and enable us to think in more nuanced ways about the haunts that shape us.

Notes on Sources:

1   The phrase is Michael Polanyi's. His concept of 'tacit knowledge' is particularly germane to this way of thinking about place. See *The Tacit Dimension* (New York: Anchor Books, 1967).

2   Dylan Trigg, *The Memory of Place: A Phenomenology of the Uncanny* (Athens: Ohio University Press, 2012), 33.

3   'Steps to an Ecology of Place', in Doreen Massey, John Allen and Philip Sarre (eds.), *Human Geography Today* (Cambridge: Polity, 1999, 295–322); 301.

4   Mary Isabella Lee, *The Not So Poor: An Autobiography*, ed. Annabel Cooper (Auckland: Auckland University Press, 1993); James Cowan, *The Old Frontier, Te Awamutu: The Story of the Waipa Valley* (Te Awamutu: Waipa Post, 1922); Keith Sinclair, *Halfway Round the Harbour* (Auckland: Penguin, 1993); Peter Wells, *Long Loop Home: A Memoir* (Auckland: Vintage, 2001). The work of mine I draw on in this essay is: introduction to *The Not So Poor*; 'Nō Ōrākau: Past and People in James Cowan's Places', *Journal of New Zealand Studies* 19 (2015): 63–78; 'Point Chev Boys and the Landscapes of Suburban Memory: Autobiographies of Auckland childhoods', *Gender, Place and Culture* 16:2 (2009), 121–38; 'On Viewing Jane Campion as an Antipodean', in H. Radner, A. Fox and I. Bessiere (eds.), *Jane Campion: Cinema, Nation, Identity* (Detroit: Wayne State University Press, 2009), 278–304.

5   All following quotes from Lee have been taken from *The Not So Poor*, 48–69.

6   Tony Ballantyne, 'Thinking Local: Knowledge, Sociability and Community in Gore's Intellectual Life, 1875–1914', *New Zealand Journal of History* 44.2 (2010) 140.

7   Te Rohe Pōtae is the 'King Country', the Kīngitanga the 'King Movement'.

8   *The New Zealand Wars: A History of the Maori Campaigns and the Pioneering Period.* (Wellington: Government Printer, 1922–23).

9   All following quotes have been taken from Cowan, *The Old Frontier*, pp. 84–95.

10   Sinclair, *Halfway Round the Harbour*.

11   Wells, *Long Loop Home*.

Place is a persistent theme in **Annabel Cooper**'s research. She has plotted gender and poverty in Dunedin's southern suburbs, mapped Dunedin's first public toilets, analysed boyhoods in Point Chevalier, traced the antipodean in the films of Jane Campion, followed road-making in Te Urewera and dug into the farming landscape at Ōrākau. Annabel's current research on cultural memory and the New Zealand Wars investigates, among other things, the significance of location in screen narratives of colonial conflict. She is an associate professor at the University of Otago.

Where the Road Leads: Place and Melodrama

Alex Calder

Sarah and I spent Labour Weekend at Mainholm Lodge, a boutique bed and breakfast miles from anywhere, in the rolling Southland hills about a half hour from Gore. Our friend Linda had recommended it advisedly—it's lovely, she said, but then she and her family were in the district for a family reunion, and she wondered if it might have been a little too much like nowhere for we Aucklanders. No wineries, no bike trails, no classic walks. But we weren't on that sort of trip—with just a couple of nights up our sleeves, we were happy enough to swap the scenery for breakfast-plus-dinner at a small country inn, and besides, we both had a power of reading to get through.

I was hoping to make progress on a piece about classic New Zealand fiction from the 1930s and 40s for a forthcoming literary history. Going back to those old books would be like a return to the heartland. It would mean coming to terms, once again, with ideas about home and place that were foundational to writers of that generation. Frank Sargeson and Allen Curnow wanted to discover what was local, special and real about place; their aversion to the way a bone-headed Kiwi triumphalism joined, in the culture of their day, with a cringing deference to anything from overseas, seemed newly relevant in the age of John Key. I would also be visiting the unvisited. The library holds shelf after shelf of minor fiction by half-forgotten authors from the 30s and 40s. Truth to tell, the prospect of reading my way through them just about matched my expectations of a holiday weekend in the vicinity of one of Southland's smaller towns. Like the tourist destinations, the fabled literary places of the south were a few hours' drive in any other direction: the Matukituki, the Maniototo or Oamaru, where Janet Frame had, as a child, yearned for 'an imagination that would inhabit a world of fact' and 'descend like a shining light upon the ordinary life of Eden Street', on her own place rather than a spurious 'elsewhere'.[1]

Eudora Welty once asked: 'what makes a given dot on the map come passionately alive, for good and all, in a novel—like one of those novae that suddenly blaze with inexplicable fire in the heavens? What brought a *Wuthering Heights* out of Yorkshire, or a *Sound and the Fury* out of Mississippi?'[2] Anyone who comes from a no-account kind of place will sense the wonder behind that question—but has it an answer? All places might be ordinary, waiting like indeterminate lumps for a Brontë, Frame or Faulkner to bring the transformative light. Or was it the other way round? Any place might be extraordinary if only we knew it. Perhaps a place called out for its story like a lost twin calling across a moor? It was with barely formulated inklings that I threw some books in a bag and caught a flight to join Sarah in Dunedin.

If you are driving over to Mainholm, the directions are simple: follow State Highway 1 until you reach the turn-off to Tapanui; take that road for 20 km or so and it's on your right. Switching on the satnav, I invited our friend the confident Australian woman to take us there. She started off plausibly enough, but our rental

Corolla was soon diverted onto a series of unsealed, insurance-voiding roads. Not to worry, we assured ourselves, the shortcut would end soon. Imagine an endless winding dusty road driven by a dairy truck on its late afternoon run—we followed several trucks down several such roads. We followed the last until the very end, until it became more riverbed than road. Below us, the boulder-strewn gorge of a roiling torrent; ahead, pine forest thickening. We shuddered up and down the hairpin loops of a logging trail until, at long last, having reached the edge of what the Australian woman called Mount Kilimanjaro, we rejoined the tarsealed road and were told to expect our destination 'in 600 m on the right'. I won't repeat what I said that afternoon, but there is a reason why my sense of injury may have been theatrically disproportionate. This was an insult stabbed right at the heart of any understanding of place. 'The map is not the territory.' Alfred Korzybski knew that. I knew that. But why couldn't that Australian woman know it too?

Mainholm was a late indulgence of the old Scotsman who first farmed the valley between the Pomohaka River and the Blue Mountains. The house is not baronial but nor is it the usual farmhouse villa or bungalow of the region. It is an elegant two-storey brick residence that looks as if it has been uplifted from a wealthy Dunedin suburb and set down in the countryside. Built in 1907, it gradually declined from family residence, to summer house, to ruin. In the 1980s, two enterprising filmmakers, Trishia Downie and John Day, bought the old place and decided to make a movie there. *The Returning*, shot in 1990, is not one of New Zealand's most distinguished films, but this supernatural thriller is memorialised in the name of the room where we slept, and where, in the fiction of the movie, a young Auckland lawyer, returning to his family's old estate, enjoys steamy congress with a ghost from the house's Victorian past. Our gracious host was keen for us to watch the DVD, and left us to it in front of a crackling fire. I have to confess we fast-forwarded through much of it, but it was obvious where the plot was headed. The lawyer begins an obsessive search into the past and yearns to join his astral lover—in a spooky closing sequence, his drowned body is pulled from the Mataura River.

Mainholm, evidently, is a place. It is where the roads lead. But Mainholm is equally the name of a place, drawing on figurative connotations of hearth and home as well as the original proprietor's fondness for the hills and valleys of Mainholm in his native South Ayrshire. Place disturbs Korzybski's rule: it is both map and territory, both a naming and the named. So many words to do with place have this doubleness. Topography hovers ambiguously between the graphic representation of a place and the contours and features so delineated. A plot of land is both the ground itself and the measuring that defines it. A plot can also mean the shaping of a narrative line, yet no plot can be elaborated without some representation of a space in which characters exist and action occurs. We usually call this a setting—the 'where and when' of a narrative according to my high-school definition—but the relation between places we might visit and places we might read about is far less straightforward than we might suppose.

When Mainholm became part of a movie, the house itself took on the related but distinct attributes of site, set and setting. Most plays or movies require a set—it might be a space set aside for performance, like a studio or theatrical stage; it can also be a location. A set is a prepared locus on which a story is about to take place, and as such can be read back from the evidence of the film or text itself. There are physical items of set such as furniture, costumes, lighting and so forth, and these manifest a cluster of intentions and dispositions. For example, an early scene in *The Returning* shows our bedroom in what would have been its dangerously dilapidated immediate post-purchase state, with sagging waterlogged ceiling and wallpaper peeling from the walls. Yet in the film, we very soon see that same room in the full glory of its restoration. What is the relation between a private home restoration project and the feature film? Is the state of our tax law circa 1990 legible in this set?—I could not possibly say. A second example: there is a peculiar blue light in the film's writhing nude scenes. The viewer understands the light is meant to emanate from the spirit world, but its use on the set also signals an aesthetic disposition. This is not blue-movie blue but R16 blue; it signifies 'erotic' in a tasteful, classy way. Reading for set in film and theatre is perhaps familiar enough, but we can approach the dramatic action of narrative fiction that way too: the representation of place in fiction is in some respects like the theatrical use of a set or the cinematic use of a location.

Considered as a site, Mainholm has a history and an address on Pomohaka Road; considered as a location, it became a set for *The Returning*, but as a setting, the old house became something else again: a venue hospitable to the telling of a certain kind of story. All settings involve cultural knowledge about the fit between storytelling and place. Take a ghost story: any writer is likely to follow—or pointedly ignore—a number of taken-for-granted but not always obvious rules. In order for a house to be haunted, it should be remote, have the functional equivalents of attic and cellar as well as everyday living spaces, and its ghost should voice wrongs from the past. In its decrepit state, Mainholm may have seemed eminently suited for a ghost story, but settings, alas, are also like tired metaphors: they lose their magic and can require a good deal of renovation. *Psycho*, for example, features a crumbling mansion atop a hill, but it took the brick veneer and neon sign of an American strip motel to revitalise that old-world gothic setting. Unlike David Ballantyne's ruined freezing works or Ronald Hugh Morrieson's water-tower, I suspect Mainholm was always going to be wrong for Kiwi gothic. It didn't call out for a ghost: it wanted a country-house murder and Inspector Poirot.

Settings, rather like dreams, have an oblique and condensed relation to the places of everyday life and to the 'hard facts' of history.[3] 'It's just a bach,' begins a well-known television advertisement, but the beach-side cottage with its long verandah and kikuyu grass lawn is a compressed and idealised version of multifarious longings and actions. Or take the beach of European landfall: as actual sites, the beaches of the Bay of Islands were spaces across which intricate and subtle cross-cultural interactions occurred, but the beach as represented in a 19th century historical painting or a mid-20th-century poem or an everyday travel brochure is a simplified projection of our feelings about what such places and events have come to mean. Our history gathers into a relatively small number of these resonant settings. Besides the beach, our more significant settings would include the bush, the farm, the marae, the suburban house, the nascent city and—a setting I didn't actually explore in *The Settler's Plot*—the small rural town.[4] Much of *The Returning* takes place in Mainholm, but we often see the protagonist driving to a rendezvous in the nearest small town: Gore, one supposes, but Gore as a setting whose primary function is to manifest and focus the sour puritanism of our settler ancestors.

A shift in setting is often the cue for a shift in style. For example, in William Satchell's novel *The Greenstone Door*, a move from Governor Grey's Auckland to the Kīngitanga pā at Pirongia is signalled by a shift from realism to the archaic diction of historical romance. The stylistic shifts disclose borderlines that can be mapped and are suggestive in terms of the relation between imagined space and historical space. If we were to focus on *The Returning* as a small-town text rather than an erotic supernatural thriller, we might notice that when it crosses a boundary from the house to the town, there is a stylistic jump from the gothic into what might look and sound like realism but is more like melodrama. This is not a weakness but an example of setting staying true to form. To explain why, let me introduce a richer example from the literature of the 1940s: Dan Davin's *Roads from Home*, which, happily for this discussion, takes place down the road from Mainholm, in Invercargill and its rural hinterland.[5]

The roads from home of the title are, first, those the older characters have taken in emigrating from the poverty of rural Ireland, and second, those of their children, who each need to find a road that will lead them away from the stultifying Catholicism of the matriarch of the family, who would crush them all with her anxious love. The book has been praised for its depiction of the 'social pattern' of mid-century New Zealand—indeed, Bob Chapman refers to it often in his famous essay.[6] For Lawrence Jones, *Roads from Home* is a regional provincial history, comparable to *Middlemarch* or *Dubliners* in its realism, its acute sense of place and in its analysis of the constrictions of small-town life by a writer who no longer shares the religious values he or she grew up with.[7]

For me, it became one of those 'unvisited' books I never got around to reading because it seemed I had been to its grim little towns too often before. But actually being on those roads has helped me view Davin's masterpiece differently. The standard line on *Roads from Home* is that the realism is excellent but not sustained: the ending, in particular, 'lacks credibility', is 'contrived', 'unconvincing' and has 'more than a touch of Hollywood'.[8] But this melodramatic quality is precisely what is best about the novel. This is not the time to develop a theory of melodrama, a mode Peter Brooks has done so much to rehabilitate, but suffice to say it flourishes in periods where there is a disconnect between society's codes of conduct and a more urgent, elemental perception of life's choices.[9] It is not unlike being misled by the satnav. When all the instructions you are given, all the familiar social clues and directions, are out of kilter with a reality people are failing to acknowledge, you might well raise your voice, you might well gesture heavenwards with your arms, and you do so because you can no longer stand the pretence: it is time something true had a voice. And it dawned on me that this was the situation of our best writers in the 1930s and 40s: writers we more often associate with realism and the nationalist search for a cultural identity. They were certainly concerned with the meanings of place, but I thought in their writing they were also particularly given to melodramatic scenes of violence and recognition, to the unblocking of necessary speech.

Lawrence Jones writes:

> The most obvious aspect of Davin's regionalism is his use of actual places in Southland. The text is sprinkled with Southland place names—Esk Street, Dee Street, Oteramika Road, Gore, Waimatua, Woodlands, Tuatapere, Wallacetown, and, as with the works of Thomas Hardy or Joyce, the reader feels in need of maps, three of which have been provided in this edition.[10]

When you first turn in to Mainholm, the driveway doubles back along the raised banks of the old railway line. On one of those maps Lawrence Jones supplies in his edition of *Roads from Home*, it is the very line that runs from Heriot, through Tapanui, Waipahi, Gore and points south, to Invercargill. The climax of the novel occurs after several of the characters have spent the day at the Gore races. The adulterous Elsie and her flashy lover, Andy, now disillusioned with each other, are driving back in his father's powerful Buick. John, her staid but decent husband, whom Elsie has tauntingly suggested is not the father of their child, is fireman on the train bringing the racegoers home. Andy has been sinking whisky throughout the day and wants to get Elsie home in time for the decencies to be preserved.

Picture the scene: we are on winding country roads and it is dark. The speeding car skids into the gravel, Andy's hands grip the wheel, and on a long straight the train is visible ahead. He accelerates, overtaking the lit carriages one by one before road and track diverge. The lovers speed on into the night. They pass Mill Road, they turn into Rockdale Road, rushing past the high macrocarpa hedges towards a level crossing on the outskirts of town:

> The hedge on [Elsie's] left stopped suddenly, revealing the express. It was on them, the headlight huge and high in its breast.
>
> 'It's John!' she screamed.
>
> Too late to brake. He forced down the accelerator till his foot was hard on the floor.
>
> The cowcatcher, like a hand, scooped up the car and tossed it into the beam. The iron breast of the engine smashed into their steel and glass.[11]

Nowadays, there is an overbridge on Rockdale Road, but older residents would recognise the name Davin gives it in his novel: Cemetery Crossing. Indeed, the novel is remarkable for its fidelity to place: thanks to Jones's maps, one can readily follow a character from Esk Street to Tay Street to the Catholic Basilica on Tyne Street. But Cemetery Crossing is also a site where destinies cross and where plot is articulated by place. Keep in mind for a moment that this is a regular small-town novel: the characters do not express themselves and there is a lot of free indirect style. After the accident, someone says: 'Well, words won't help and there's no more to be said'.[12] But sometimes place itself can speak volumes. You won't find these words on any page of the novel, but we can imagine Cemetery Crossing as a set on which Elsie, pulled from the wreckage of the car, yet strangely radiant of face, lifts a trembling arm toward her husband and says: 'You are the father of our child.'

'I forgive you, don't die', sobs John; 'I'll see you both in hell!' croaks Andy, corpsing on the cattlestop.

'All plots tend to move deathward,' says a character in Don Delillo's *White Noise*.[13] In that sense, it is no accident that leads *Roads from Home* to an unprotected level crossing, but an over-determination of the novelistic possibilities of place. In our small-town settings, words won't help and there's often nothing more to be said, but that is only because we know where the roads lead: to Cemetery Crossing, an over-the-top toponym, where place itself can be the voice of the melodrama.

Notes on Sources:

1   Janet Frame, *An Autobiography* (Auckland: Century Hutchinson, 1989), 101.

2   Eudora Welty, 'Place in Fiction', *Stories, Essays and Memoir* (New York: Library of America, 1998), 787.

3   I owe much of my thinking about setting to Philip Fisher's excellent study, *Hard Facts: Setting and Form in American Literature* (New York: Oxford University Press, 1985). The paragraph that follows paraphrases points made in his theoretical introduction, 9.

4   I discuss these and other settings in my book *The Settler's Plot: How Stories Take Place in New Zealand* (Auckland: Auckland University Press, 2011).

5   Dan Davin, *Roads From Home* (1949) ed. Lawrence Jones, (Auckland: Auckland University Press, 1976), vii–xix.

6   Robert Chapman, 'Fiction and the Social Pattern', *Landfall* 25 (1953) 26–52.

7   Lawrence Jones, 'Introduction', *Roads From Home*, vii-xix.

8   The quoted phrases combine citations from reviewers with Jones's own comments in his introduction to the novel, xvii–xviii.

9   See Peter Brooks, *The Melodramatic Imagination: Balzac, Henry James, Melodrama* and the Mode of Excess, 2nd ed. (New Haven: Yale University Press, 1995).

10   Jones, 'Introduction', viii.

11   *Roads from Home*, 234.

12   *Roads from Home*, 247.

13   Don Delillo, *White Noise*, (New York: Penguin Classics, 2009), 26.

Alex Calder is an associate professor and the Head of English, Drama and Writing Studies at the University of Auckland. He currently teaches courses in New Zealand literature, the writings of Herman Melville and Joseph Conrad, the gothic, and literary theory and critical practice. His research, for which he has received a Marsden award, focuses on processes of cultural contact and settlement, particularly with regard to writings from New Zealand and the United States. His most recent book is *The Settler's Plot: How Stories Take Place in New Zealand* (Auckland University Press, 2011).

On the Road to Nowhere: Revisiting Samuel Butler's *Erewhon*

Jack Ross

Over the Range

The Erewhonians say that we are drawn through life backwards; or again, that we go onwards into the future as into a dark corridor. Time walks beside us and flings back shutters as we advance; but the light thus given often dazzles us, and deepens the darkness which is in front. We can see but little at a time, and heed that little far less than our apprehension of what we shall see next . . .

—Samuel Butler, *Erewhon*[1]

Samuel Butler's *Erewhon* is, literally, nowhere: an inversion of Utopia, Thomas More's imaginary state in (or near) South America. It is, however, *reachable* from somewhere—or rather, from *Erewhemos*, the state contiguous to Erewhon described at the end of its 1901 sequel, *Erewhon Revisited*.

People often forget that the subtitle of *Erewhon* is 'Over the Range.' I have in my mind's eye the cover of the mid-1970s edition of *Erewhon*, in the Golden Press series of New Zealand classics. It shows a lone rider in a Southern Alpine landscape—a detail from a 19th-century realist landscape painting called 'The Waimakariri River Bed'.[2] This image, evoking the mood of James K. Baxter's 'High Country Weather' ('Upon the upland road/ Ride easy, stranger'), certainly had the effect of reinscribing the story's New Zealand setting in *my* imagination when I first came across it as a teenager.

As a born-and-bred Aucklander, I had few associations with the South Island and the Canterbury Plains beyond a few family camping trips. My father lived in Templeton, outside Christchurch, for a single year during his childhood, but his principal memory seemed to be of the long straight roads, with deep drainage ditches on either side, which my grandfather would cycle along—his two boys taking turns to ride pillion behind him.

Nevertheless, when I came across the following description of Erewhon in Alberto Manguel and Gianni Guadalupi's otherwise authoritative *Dictionary of Imaginary Places* (1980), I felt almost offended:

> ...a kingdom *probably in central or northern Australia* [my emphasis], though its location has been deliberately concealed by travellers who have visited it. Those geographers who have placed it in New Zealand (Upper Rangitata district, Canterbury) have not taken into account the sheer immensity of its land surface.[3]

Given the deliberately over-literal and tongue-in-cheek nature of Manguel and Guadalupi's book, it would be silly to resent too strongly their reassignment of Erewhon to our larger, brasher neighbour (though precedents such as Pavlova, Phar Lap and Crowded House do spring to mind). It still seems a bit odd, though, that a place so unequivocally *nowhere* should have to be so firmly located *somewhere*.

Perhaps that subtitle 'Over the Range' becomes particularly significant here. It denotes movement from *here* to *there*, from the known to the unknown, from the closely observed (by Butler himself, among others) Canterbury of the 1860s, to the Otherwhere of the imagination.

We need to go somewhere else to see where we've been: to the unknown place to look back on what we thought we knew. And, like all binaries, this dichotomy between nowhere and somewhere, Erewhon and Erewhemos, suggests something in between: the true subject of investigation, albeit one which can only be taken by surprise, as in a Knight's move.

Arthur's Pass

An old friend of mine, whom I'll be calling Graeme for the purposes of this essay, owned a bach in Arthur's Pass for a few years in the late 1990s. We were close at school and university, but I'd seen little of him since he moved to the small Canterbury town of Darfield to work as their rural GP.

I only visited his bach (or should I say 'crib'?) once, for a single night. I'd often wondered why he talked about it so much, and went to such extraordinary lengths to get there. From the road it looked like nothing much: a rough discoloured shed with walls of corrugated iron.

But then I walked inside and saw the view.

It's not that it was particularly grandiose: no Albert Bierstadt ranges of snowy mountains towering up into infinity. Rather, it was the more intimate charm of forest and valley, with a single rocky stream. When I awoke next morning, the fog had already rolled in.

Graeme had gone for a walk, and I was left alone in the cabin. I looked out the window at the trees looming through the mist, and felt a kind of joy at the perfection of this place, a mood of quiet contentment such as I hardly remember experiencing anywhere else.

'This would make the perfect location for a writers' retreat,' I thought, and later, after we'd driven back down to the Plains, hinted as much to Graeme. He didn't take the bait. I never succeeded in making my way back there again—though not for want of trying.

Later, when he moved down to Dunedin after a marriage breakup, he was forced to sell it in order to make up the price of a house deposit. I'm sure he's regretted it many times since—as have I. Perhaps it couldn't have lived up to that miraculous first impression if I'd gone back there later, on my own, but I doubt that. It was just a magical spot, a place of peace and refreshment.

My friend and Christchurch poet John O'Connor once told me of an experience he'd had during his teens, when he and a few friends drove out of the city and the working-class suburb he'd grown up in, and stopped for a short walk in the hills on the way to Arthur's Pass.

The others got bored quite fast, he said, but (as he put it), 'I felt like I wanted to sing, as if I couldn't believe anything could possibly be so beautiful.' John died earlier this year, but I can't help remembering that story whenever I think about Canterbury and the Southern Alps.

The statues

> A few steps brought me nearer, and a shudder of unutterable horror ran through me when I saw a circle of gigantic forms, many times higher than myself, upstanding grim and grey through the veil of cloud before me.

One of the strangest things in *Erewhon* (not to mention its sequel) are the repeated references to the ring of statues which guard the unnamed colony the narrator lives in from the imaginary country which borders it: 'a sort of

Stonehenge of rude and barbaric figures . . . [with a] superhumanly malevolent expression upon their faces.'

It actually takes the narrator some time to realise that these 'were not living beings, but statues'.

> They were barbarous—neither Egyptian, nor Assyrian, nor Japanese— different from any of these, and yet akin to all. They were six or seven times larger than life, of great antiquity, worn and lichen-grown. They were ten in number.

What's more, not only do they *look* forbidding—'Each was terrible after a different kind. One was raging furiously, as in pain and great despair; another was lean and cadaverous with famine; another cruel and idiotic'—but they *sound* frightening, too:

> The inhuman beings into whose hearts the Evil One had put it to conceive these statues, had made their heads into a sort of organ-pipe, so that their mouths should catch the wind and sound with its blowing. It was horrible. However brave a man might be, he could never stand such a concert, from such lips and in such a place. [4]

In narrative terms, too, one could say that these figures constitute a barrier: between the circumstantial verisimilitude of his opening chapters, so clearly drawn from Butler's own observations of the Canterbury colony (as recorded in his 1863 book *A First Year in Canterbury Settlement*)[5] and the fantastic inversions which characterise the no-place his protagonist would shortly enter.

The cautery

It was the early 90s. I'd been at an academic conference in Dunedin, and thought I'd take the opportunity to drop in on Graeme on my way home. I accordingly took the bus from Dunedin to Christchurch, which was (in retrospect) a pretty stupid thing to do.

Tempers were already wearing thin when I came rolling into the depot a couple of hours late—due to various misadventures on the way— and I could see that Graeme's family could probably have done without this lengthy interruption to their day. So tense, in fact, was the atmosphere on the way back to his place that I began to wonder if it would even be possible to last out the weekend I'd budgeted on staying.

I mentioned to Graeme, more to make conversation than anything else, that I'd been having trouble with nosebleeds all through my stay in Dunedin, and had had to run out of a couple of sessions with blood on my shirt and two fingers pinched shut on my nasal passages.

Nothing could be easier to fix, he told me. He could cauterise my nose: seal shut the vein which must be causing the problem. He had the tools to hand in his surgery down the road.

Since both of my parents were GPs, I'd got into the bad habit of relying on family and friends for medical advice, and—as the youngest of three brothers—had (in any case) a certain ingrained tendency to see doctors as authority figures. Reluctant though I was to go along with this plan, I let him persuade me to climb back into the car.

It was long after hours, and we were the only ones in the surgery. It was a modern pre-fab, but the garish religious pamphlets and posters which his partner, an evangelical Christian, had left lying around the place gave it a strange gothic atmosphere. He told me to strip, then strapped me down on the table ('In case you flinch too much when I put it in and it ends up in the wrong place.')

The cautery, the small metal rod he was proposing to stick up my nose, took a while to heat up, and—in the meantime—he took a good look up my nostril to see the exposed vein. It was, it seemed, quite visible and ready to be seared shut.

The process was quite intrusive (as you might expect): not directly painful, exactly, but certainly *very* uncomfortable. Nor is snuffing the scent of one's own scorched flesh ever exactly pleasant.

I did think of some things while I lay there, though. What was I *doing* there, for one thing? Why had I agreed to this bizarre procedure in the first place? 'Never again, under any circumstances,' was my main thought. The next was to wonder how many more minutes I would have to endure before I could leave.

After that trip we didn't make contact again for several years.

Leap, John, leap!

However peculiar *Erewhon* may seem to contemporary readers, so many of the attitudes and controversies it mocks having faded away over the intervening century and a half, *Erewhon Revisited* is stranger.

Even the way it's told, a deathbed account by 'George Higgs' (the original narrator, named now for the first time) of his return to Erewhon, recounted secondhand by his son John, seems so diffuse and clumsy as to call into question the accuracy of *everything* that's being reported.

Perhaps this was originally designed as a sly dig at the authenticity of the Gospels—the main target of Butler's satire this time round—but it ends up sounding more like a tribute to other *fin-de-siècle* novels by the likes of Conrad and James, with their unreliable narrators and obsession with the vagaries of human psychology.

Even the ring of statues appears to have changed in the intervening twenty years. His English-born son John reports that his father found them 'smaller than he had expected':

> He had said in his book—written many months after he had seen them—that they were about six times the size of life, but he now thought that four or five times would have been enough to say.

But if these statues had 'grown' in his imagination, what of the far more startling discoveries he had made in Erewhon itself? Were those to be called into question, too? Certain other important aspects of their appearance seem curiously altered, also:

> Their mouths were much clogged with snow, so that even though there had been a strong wind (which there was not) they would not have chanted.

The statues recur in the story when Higgs is being assisted in his escape over the range by his newly encountered Erewhonian son George: 'Towards noon they caught sight of the statues and a halt was made which gave my father the first pang he had felt that morning, for he knew that the statues would be the beginning of the end.' Higgs and his son do, however, make a 'solemn covenant' at the statues that they will meet again:

> XXI. i. 3, *i.e.* our December 9, 1891, I am to meet George at the statues, at twelve o'clock, and if he does not come, I am to be there again on the following day.

Higgs adds one proviso: 'if I cannot come I will send your brother.'

The next chapter of the book, however, is headed 'My Father reaches Home, and Dies not long Afterwards.'

John is nevertheless determined to meet his long-lost Erewhonian brother, and travels out to the colonies to try to make this rendezvous. He finally succeeds in reaching the statues on the appointed day, but 'could not refrain from some disappointment at finding them a good deal smaller than I had expected':

> My father, correcting the measurement he had given in his book, said he thought that they were about four or five times the size of life; but

really I don't think they were more than twenty feet high, any one of them . . . There was no wind, and as matter of course, therefore, they were not chanting.

This constant insistence that they are somehow *reducing in size*—from the 40 or 50 feet of the first estimate, to the 30-odd feet of the second, to no 'more than twenty feet high, any one of them'—seems a curious point to stress, even in context. Why, too, should their *failure* to chant be considered such a 'matter of course'?

> . . . when sleep came it was accompanied by a strange dream. I dreamed that I was by my father's bedside, watching his last flicker of intelligence, and vainly trying to catch the words that he was not less vainly trying to utter. All of a sudden the bed seemed to be at my camping-ground, and the largest of the statues appeared, quite small, high up the mountain side, but striding down like a giant in seven-league boots till it stood over me and my father, and shouted out, 'Leap, John, leap!' In the horror of this vision I woke.[6]

The meeting of the two brothers takes place a day late, due to the fact that 'the year XX had been a leap year with the Erewhonians, and 1891 in England had not.' This, it appears, is the true meaning behind that strange cry in his dream: 'Leap, John, leap!' Our narrator also remarks that 'George gained an immediate ascendancy over me, but ascendancy is not the word—he took me by storm; how, or why, I neither know nor want to know.'

Disproportionate emphasis is, I think, the predominant impression given by the constant recurrence of these statues in Butler's two books about Erewhon. They are (we are told initially) 'terrible,' 'barbarous,'—*and* musical, but only in a 'horrible' way. Their size, moreover, seems to fluctuate inexplicably.

Either, one is forced to conclude, they serve as a rather redundant addition to Butler's otherwise fairly straightforward satire on the *mores* and opinions of Victorian England, or they have some other function in his narrative, express some anxiety which cannot find a clearer voice there.

North East Valley

Last year I visited Graeme again, this time at his house in North East Valley, Dunedin.

I'd stayed there before a couple of times, and had watched its gradual decline from a basically functional living space—albeit with a few too many boxes stacked in odd corners—into a warren of unread papers and books. Even so, seeing it now came as a bit of a shock.

The steeply sloping section was completely overgrown. The lawn had been left unmown for so long that the grass was higher than my waist. Neighbourhood cats had scoured tunnels through the high grass, and mewed in protest as I tried to beat a way up along the path.

I'd warned him what time I'd be arriving, but even so there was no answer to my repeated knocking and ringing of the bell at the back door. In desperation, I made the long, perilous journey to the *front* door, which had not been used for years, and could only be reached by pushing right through the heart of the jungle.

No answer there, either: I could see that there was a light on inside, but the porch was overgrown and dusty, with an old rotting cushion disintegrating on one of the wicker chairs.

I made my way back. Eventually, after further knocking, he *did* answer the door, explaining that he'd been listening to the radio and had lost track of time.

It didn't look as if there had been any attempt to tidy up in advance of my visit, but Graeme claimed this was not the case—that if I'd come to the house a week or so before I'd have found it impossible to move from room to room.

He admitted to suffering from a lack of energy and motivation, and even to the probability that one might have to describe this condition as a kind of depression. He did not, however, think that treatment or counselling would be likely to help ('There are so many factors involved, most of which they wouldn't be able to help with').

The visit cannot be said to have gone well. I learned quite quickly that it was unwise to let him drive me anywhere (he had a habit of overtaking trucks on blind corners which was disconcerting, to say the least). It was his behaviour in public which was really awkward, though.

On the one occasion we went out to dinner together, he distinguished himself by dropping his fork on the floor and demanding a clean one to replace it. No sooner had the new one arrived than he dropped *that* on the floor, too—or, rather, catapulted it there while banging the table to emphasise some loud point he was making. He was about to call out for a new one when he caught my eye. After that he contented himself with making an immense fuss over the amount of butter they'd put on the naan bread, then complaining about the dessert.

His property in the valley was a couple of blocks down from that 'steepest street in the world' which the local scarfies like to roll down in wheelie bins (until one of them got killed doing it, that is). It's a beautiful spot, with a great view of the wooded hills opposite, and even a certain amount of sunlight—for Dunedin.

As for the house itself, it's well-built and sound, though certainly suffering from neglect. Before flying out, I took the gamble of doing some *tidying up*: pinning up a few of the beautiful Indonesian and Indian artefacts Graeme had picked up in his travels, purging a few hundred kgs of old magazines and waste paper, and rearranging his lounge and dining room so one had space to sit down in them.

Graeme seemed quite grateful that I'd taken the trouble, which was a relief. People don't always like you to go sorting through their stuff while they're out for the day. Who knows what you might find?

A Field Guide to the Other World

I remember once trying to explain to the arch-sceptic Graeme my interest in occultism and the supernatural. I'd just been reading Patrick Harpur's *Daimonic Reality: A Field Guide to the Other World*, so I tried to account for this fascination using one of Harpur's paradigms:

> The Otherworld mirrors ours. It can be benign, like the paradises that reverse this world's suffering; or it can be uncanny, like the realm some tribes ascribe to witches who walk or talk backwards, wear their heads upside down, their legs back to front.[7]

What better analogy could one find to Erewhon? Its names—'Senoj Nosnibor, Ydgrun, Thims'—that run backwards; its location in the Antipodes where *everything* is 'upside down'; even its clothes worn, like Professor Panky's, 'like an Englishman . . . but turned the wrong way round, so that when his face was towards my father his body seemed to have its back towards him and *vice versa*'?[8]

The basic point of Harpur's book, I told Graeme, was to postulate a 'daimonic reality' which exists—either literally or psychologically (Harpur sees little distinction between the two)—as a contrast to our world of causation and certainty. Ghosts, poltergeists, UFOs, lake monsters, Bigfoot, the yeti, fairies, angels, demons all inhabit this reality, but not—for the most part—*as we see them*.

The 'glamour' which these beings are able to throw across the perceptions of mortals who chance into this uncanny sphere means that the size, shape and essential nature of all that they see there, including its inhabitants, is always open to question: hence Harpur's contention that the description of a haunting and a UFO abduction narrative may be basically the same thing.

This approach is indebted to C.G. Jung's classic *Flying Saucers: A Modern Myth of Things Seen in the Sky*, where the Swiss psychologist sets to one side the question of the objective existence of such phenomena, but rather looks into the psychological implications of this transformation of the more traditional apparitions of folklore into spaceships and aliens. Fear was behind it, he concluded: anxiety over the atom bomb and the accelerating rate of post-war technological change.

Harpur, too, wishes to see some larger significance in the exponentially multiplying field of anecdotal and analytical accounts of paranormal events. The fact that people continue to experience such things and to ascribe so much personal significance to these encounters and sightings is, in his view, far more important than whether they can be claimed to be 'real'.

Real in what sense? The fact that such phenomena can seldom be persuaded to recur in laboratories does not, in itself, render them 'non-existent'. Can feelings such as love, hatred or even pain be measured according to objective outside criteria? Does this make them, too, unreal?

Pain is only too real to those who suffer from it. It can come as a shock to the congenitally literal-minded to realise that the extent of *any* pain—physical or psychological—can only be determined anecdotally, by asking the person experiencing it.

My own repeated readings of Samuel Butler's *Erewhon* at different points of my life cannot be said to add to much more than a series of indeterminable questions.

Where *is* the book set? What is the true significance of the statues? Why does Butler (or rather, his narrator) stress their reduction in size over time? Why, in particular, does he take the trouble to transcribe the particular musical phrase from Handel that their moanings most resemble?

One of the few constants at all stages of my friend Graeme's life has been a love for music: choral music in particular. He's sung in choirs for many years, and can improvise effortlessly on virtually any musical instrument: pianos, recorders, organs.

I suppose, for him, this constitutes the best way to *step out of his life*: ignore the frustrations and rages which seem to haunt him like furies, and disappear into a counter-realm of order and harmony.

The composition of *Erewhon* must have served a similar purpose for Butler: a way of examining the assumptions—religious, colonialist, racist—of his upbringing: from the distance not just of the farthest point on Earth from the oppressive values of his father's rectory, but from a new world altogether. He stepped through the looking-glass into another place in order to look back. Or, as he himself puts it, in 'the world of the unborn':

> . . . we presage the leading lines of that which is before us, by faintly reflected lights from dull mirrors that are behind. [9]

For me, I suppose that this account of a few visits to the South Island is a way of talking about how the story of a friendship can mirror our feelings both about a place and the progress of a life. For me, Dunedin and the Alps are inextricably bound up with my meetings with Graeme: the original affection overlaid with a certain frustration at where he's ended up now. But it also constitutes a gauge: a mirror of the nowheres I've been, in light of the somewhere I hope I'm approaching.

Patrick Harpur's rules for travel in the Otherworld seem to ring only too true for all these contingencies:

> Travel light. Don't believe everything you've been told, either for good or ill . . . Observe local customs; respect local gods. Talk less than you listen. Try to see as well as sightsee. Be polite but firm; take advice but do not be gullible. If in doubt, smile. Do not laugh at the natives, but don't be afraid to laugh . . . Don't join in the dancing unless you really have learnt the steps. [10]

Notes on Sources:

1   Samuel Butler, *Erewhon, or Over the Range*, 1872, New Zealand Classics (Auckland: Golden Press, 1973), 156.

2   By one 'J. Attwood' (= T. R. [Thomas Reginald] Attwood) [information from Una Platts. *Nineteenth Century New Zealand Artists: A Guide and Handbook* (Christchurch: Avon Fine Prints Limited, 1980), 27. Available at: http://christchurchcitylibraries.com/Heritage/Publications/Art/Platts-19thC/Platts-19thCArtists.pdf.

3   Alberto Manguel and Gianni Guadalupi, *The Dictionary of Imaginary Places*, Illustrated by Graham Greenfield, Maps and Charts by James Cook, 1980 (London: Granada, 1981), 113.

4   This, and previous quotations in this section, come from Butler, 1973, 47–48.

5   Compiled by his father, the Reverend Thomas Butler, from essays and letters sent home, but subsequently repudiated by Butler himself, who would not allow it to be reprinted in his lifetime (information from Samuel Butler, *A First Year in Canterbury Settlement*, 1863, ed. A.C. Brassington & P.B. Maling [Auckland & Hamilton: Blackwood & Janet Paul], 1964.)

6   This, and the previous four quotations, come from Samuel Butler, *Erewhon Revisited*, The Travellers' Library, 1901 (London: Jonathan Cape, 1927), 37, 279, 281 and 301–1.

7   Patrick Harpur, *Daimonic Reality: A Field Guide to the Other World*, 1994 (Ravensdale, WA: Pine Winds Press, 2003), 174.

8   Butler, 1927, 43, 41.

9   Butler, 1973, 156.

10   Harpur, 276–77.

Jack Ross is a senior lecturer in creative writing at Massey University's Auckland campus. His latest book, *A Clearer View of the Hinterland: Poems and Sequences 1981–2014*, appeared in 2014 from HeadworX in Wellington. His other publications include four poetry collections, three novels and three volumes of short fiction. He has also edited a number of books and literary magazines, including *Poetry NZ* (from 2014). Further details can be found on his blog, *The Imaginary Museum* (http://mairangibay.blogspot.com).

Finding the Here in Elsewhere

Harry Ricketts

Tēnā koutou katoa. Ko Malvern Hills te maunga. Ko Severn te awa. No London ahau. Ko Harry Ricketts toku ingoa. Kia ora. Hello to you all, my mountain is the Malvern Hills, my river the Severn, my birthplace London, my name Harry Ricketts. That at least is one version of a mihimihi through which I could rather awkwardly introduce myself in Māori terms, and, as far as it goes, the points of identification are true, or at least not untrue. In another version, equally not untrue, Kledang Hill in Malaysia or The Peak in Hong Kong could replace the Malvern Hills, and Kinta River or Ho Chung River replace the Severn. My father was a British army officer and reposted every couple of years, so my childhood, like that of many 'fag-end of Empire kids' as my friend Nigel used to call us, was a constant series of dislocations and relocations. By ten, I had lived in London,

Malaysia, Epsom, Worcester, Hong Kong and Worcester again—not to mention two years in that other foreign country, the English prep school. Sometimes if someone, uncertain whether my accent is English or New Zealand, asks me where I come from, I just say 'The British army'; it seems as good an answer as any.

The downside of this is that I don't really have a tūrangawaewae, a standing place of the heart, and from time to time I must admit I envy those who do. It must be affirming to know where you come from, to know in your bones where you belong and to what and to whom, and to be able to state this unequivocally. Or so I like to imagine. Because another side of me is sceptical of what, in a New Zealand context, some label 'settler envy' or 'immigrant envy', detecting behind such an encapsulation feelings which are really too complicated and conflicted to be boiled down to a potentially reductive formula of the placed and displaced. (It's not who we are that's important, but who we think we are, to adapt an aphorism of the eccentric General Conyers in Anthony Powell's novel-sequence *A Dance to the Music of Time*.) For me, not having these hard-wired attachments has its advantages. Instead of home, I have a succession of what that connoisseur of migration and exile, Salman Rushdie, calls 'imaginary homelands', which through memory I can, and do, constantly revisit.[1] Actually, my imaginary homelands are more like a series of PowerPoint slides seen as though hovering a few feet above ground level: tiny, wild strawberries in the rockery; the copse behind the officers' mess; phosphorescence shining in the dark sea; lying awake, listening to the distant drone of planes leaving Heathrow; the lawn with the cricket net. So whenever I read the word 'here' (or hear it, a disquieting aural pun), it creaks like a squeaky floorboard. 'Here' is never a place open, vivid and known; it is hidden away unreachably within longer, fuzzier words like 'where', 'there', 'somewhere', 'everywhere' and particularly 'elsewhere'.

Which can be a problem, but is also full of opportunity. 'Elsewhere', for instance, is the natural location of the personal essay. 'Elsewhere' is where the personal essay can always take us, either reading it, listening to it, or trying to write it. 'Elsewhere' is also the place we can bring back to the personal essay and perhaps offer others, the 'ghostly host' to which Martin Edmond referred in his keynote address at the December 2014 *Placing the Personal Essay Colloquium* at Massey University—or should that really have been 'hostly ghost'? And think how limited, how thin, how evanescent, the word 'here' is, compared to 'elsewhere'. We have access to so many 'elsewheres' through the internet, through books, through films, through paintings, through history, through memory, through imagination. Of all these 'elsewheres', the past is for many the richest and most rewarding. Look at it stretching out behind us: 'So various, so beautiful, so new', as Matthew Arnold says of 'the world' in 'Dover Beach'.[2] But also, as he doesn't say: so similar, so ugly, so old. Which is why the past is such a natural location for the personal essay: the past is both solid and always shifting. It is wonderfully, as the opening sentence of *The Go-Between* reminds us, 'a foreign country' where they 'do things differently'; it is also, as the narrator of Tim Winton's story 'Aquifer' puts it, 'in us, and not behind us'.[3] The past is so versatile. The past—our own past and all the other pasts that comprise history and pre-history—is the puzzle we can never work out, but can never leave alone. The fluid, flexible personal essay is often valued as a vehicle of discovery, and where better to take it to make discoveries than the 'elsewhere' of the past. We will find stuff; we know that. The past is full of it: stuff about ourselves (not always reliable), stuff about others, stuff about writing, stuff about stuff.

But, as Edmond also pointed out, through the personal essay, we can do more than make discoveries, exciting and necessary as these may be. (Even writing this essay, I made a few tiny discoveries, such as noticing the convenient linguistic accident that, in English, 'here' is hidden away in 'elsewhere'.) And one of the most valuable things we can do in the personal essay is to bring the 'elsewhere' of the past back to life on the page. We can in a way, sadly the only way, bring back the 'elsewhere' of the dead like my friend Nigel, who once called us 'fag-end of Empire kids'.

I knew Nigel for 45 years; he was my oldest friend. He had a long face, stiff brown hair and heavy eyebrows always just about to shoot up at the revelation of another of life's idiosyncrasies. We first met in 1963 at school in England. We were in the same form for the next five years, and guardedly friendly—he wary of my sportiness, I of his quick wit and plausible French accent. Our friendship really began at Oxford. It was there that we found ourselves falling into the kind of uncensored conversations you only ever have with a few people. I came to realise that he was both teasing and kind, and I learnt from him that you can be playful and serious at the same time, that a shift in tone need not imply a shift in sympathy. Three summers working in a Ribena factory in Coleford near his parents' fruit farm in Herefordshire cemented the friendship. Nigel had a beaten-up Morris Traveller and would drive us to work through the five o'clock mist with the pigeons clattering up from the gravelly roads. 'Coleford,' he would say as we laboured up the final hill, 'gateway to the West!' One day in the gender- and other-bending early 1970s, we had the obligatory conversations about sex and sexuality. During one of these, he said almost as a throwaway remark: 'I think I may be bisexual.' Over the years, he would regularly tease me about my reply: 'Aren't we all?' This, I used to assume, meant that he felt I hadn't taken him and his uncertainty sufficiently seriously, but now that I can't ask him I feel far less sure.

Nigel had a keen appreciation of kitsch in all its forms and, more generally, a sense of style. When I got a job lecturing in Hong Kong, he took me to an expensive menswear shop and insisted I buy a pale blue suit with wide lapels. I suppose this very non-me get-up reflected a dress code he thought my new position required, but, compelled by his certainty, I never stopped to ask. He loved European films. After a lunch in London in 1973, he bundled me into a taxi with instructions to go straight to a cinema which was showing Truffaut's *Day for Night*. A decade or so later on a visit to the UK from New Zealand, he told me that if I wanted to understand Thatcherland, I had to see *Letter to Brezhnez* and *My Beautiful Laundrette*. Which was good advice. I sometimes used to think that for him God was a celestial movie director, preferably French.

After I moved to New Zealand in the early 1980s, we naturally saw much less of each other, and he was a famously hopeless letter-writer and, later, emailer. ('A postcard a decade, if you're lucky', as one friend used to complain.) But on visits to England I would stay with him and his Brazilian partner Fernando in their basement flat in Shepherds Bush, and the conversations would start up as though we had seen each other only the other day. On one visit, I was banging on about my recent discovery of the work of the late Bruce Chatwin. 'I used to know him a bit,' said Nigel, after I had gone on for a while about *Utz*. He had met Chatwin in the late 1970s while the latter was working on *The Viceroy of Ouidah*, his fictionalised biography of the 19th-century Brazilian-born slave trader Francisco Félix de Sousa, who became the viceroy of Ouidah in Dahomey (now Benin). Nigel had been living in Brazil, teaching at the Cultura Inglesa. By then his Portuguese was pretty fluent, and he acted as an interpreter for Chatwin, helping him with his Brazilian research. When I asked what Chatwin was like, Nigel said he was physically and mentally tough. One day when they were running to catch a bus, a small boy happened to be in the way; Chatwin, without pausing, dropped his shoulder and shoved the child aside. He carried a notebook everywhere, wrote everything down. He advised Nigel not to use too many metaphors in his writing: 'You want to get translated, don't you?' In *Under the Sun: The Letters of Bruce Chatwin*, there are two letters to Nigel from 1978, one of which asks him to help with some scraps of research in Lisbon ('like what would a Lt Colonel in the Portuguese Army be wearing in the tropics in 1875?') and offering to pay travel expenses.[4] The recent discovery and reading of these letters made me catch my breath. Nigel hadn't ever mentioned letters. Why should he? But realising that he hadn't, brought home to me in a rush how little we really know even about our close friends, and I felt rather envious.

After years as a producer for Radio 4, Nigel set up his own small production company, Loftus Productions, in 1996, and won various radio awards. It was he who first told me how good Flight of the Conchords were, having seen them at the Edinburgh Festival. He also told me, after interviewing Stephen Spender, that the old poet, recalling the 1930s, had pronounced 'Fascists' as 'Fassists', and he wondered whether that was how the word was commonly said back then. He would periodically send me cassettes of programmes he thought I might like. One was called 'Mum, I've Got Something to Tell You', about gay men coming out to their parents.

Our last conversation was in the autumn of 2007 at Pizza Express in Shepherds Bush, a favourite haunt. We talked about many things, including the rare form of stomach cancer from which he was dying and those perennial topics—families and relationships. He said he wasn't afraid to die, but wished he could have lived longer 'to see how it all worked out'. His final, teasing remark was: 'I've always envied you your certainty about your sexuality.' I couldn't get to London for his memorial service the following spring, but another old friend went and read a poem I'd written. Nigel's last words (to the person who was helping him take a drink through a straw) were, characteristically: 'Are *you* all right?'

One of our recurring topics over the years was an imaginary homeland of Nigel's, Iquique in Chile. It's a place with a complicated colonial history, and, for Nigel, its particular appeal was that his family had made money there during the sodium nitrate boom before having to decamp hastily back to England where they struggled to keep up appearances in genteel Cheltenham. This kind of story with its class and other nuances always fascinated him, and he did a good deal of research on Iquique and his family's involvement there, and I think made a radio documentary based on what he discovered. It was presumably in part Iquique that drew him to South America in the first place, and caused him to meet Fernando. If so, the search for an 'elsewhere' in the past eventually led to a real place, a 'here' in the present, when he and Fernando moved to England and established a life together in Shepherds Bush. As for me, I've lived in Wellington for 34 years, more than half my life, in a succession of flats and houses; two of my children live here, and my second wife is a New Zealander. That ought to count for something, to affirm some sort of 'here' in the 'elsewhere', to prompt a further recasting of my mihimihi.

Notes on Sources:

1   Salman Rushdie, 'Imaginary Homelands' in *Imaginary Homelands: Essays and Criticism 1981-1991* (London: Granta Books in association with Penguin Books, 1991), 9–21.
2   Kenneth Allott (ed), *The Poems of Matthew Arnold* (London: Longmans, 1965), 242.
3   L. P. Hartley, *The Go-Between* (London: Hamish Hamilton, 1953), 9; Tim Winton, 'Aquifer', in *The Turning* (Sydney: Picador, 2004), 53.
4   Elizabeth Chatwin and Nicholas Shakespeare (eds.), Under the Sun: *The Letters of Bruce Chatwin* (New York: Viking Penguin, 2011), 301.

Harry Ricketts teaches English literature and creative nonfiction at Victoria University of Wellington. His 30 books include 10 collections of poems, two literary biographies and two extended personal essays. *How to Live Elsewhere* (Four Winds Press, 2004) reflects on a peripatetic childhood spent in the UK, Malaysia and Hong Kong, and later ricochetings which led to coming to live in New Zealand in 1981. *How to Catch a Cricket Match* (Awa, 2006) is organised around a single day's play during a Test between New Zealand and the West Indies in Wellington in March 2006. The book blends cricket history, literature and instruction with personal reminiscence, and is a gappy autobiography of sorts. It has been reprinted and broadcast a number of times on National Radio. In 2014 a shorter personal essay, 'On Masks and Migration', appeared in the 'Pacific Highways' issue of the *Griffith Review*.

The [taniwha] of Poplar Avenue

Lynn Jenner

In September 2014 I met a young Māori man working on the MacKays to Peka Peka Kāpiti Expressway. At some point in my conversation with him the thought came to me that he had a taniwha CLIMBING UP HIS NECK.

From now on this taniwha will appear in my text in brackets to make it crystal clear that if there is a taniwha of the waterways between the hills and the sea, near the intersection of State Highway 1 and Poplar Avenue, he probably would not reveal himself to me.

That afternoon I had been photographing signs at the gate of the Poplar Avenue construction site. I had focused my camera on a list of hazards, a needle pointing to the need for visitors to go to the office and the full names and cellphone numbers of Dave and Mike, the men who are in charge of the site. Delivery of yellow rock, for example, was an ongoing hazard, and had been since late July 2014, when the sign had last been updated.

A white sedan pulled up beside me. The driver, a young man of perhaps twenty or twenty-five, asked me very politely what I was doing there.

'Just having a look,' I said. 'Don't worry. I'm just looking at how fast things are changing. I'll stay on my side of the fence.'

'Are you from the street over there?' the young man asked, pointing to Leinster Avenue. Leinster Avenue had fairly recently been closed to traffic. Several houses had been compulsorily purchased and then moved away on trucks or demolished. Several others were on the market and had been for months, because who would buy a house next to an Expressway?

'No,' I said. 'I'm from further down, near the sea.' I waved my arm airily towards the west. So there we were. Him, leaning on the car, asking what I later came to recognise as the standard Alliance[1] conversation opener. Me, keeping my opinions to myself. Despite this I felt a rope around me. There was plenty to spare, but someone was holding it, feeding it out.[2]

I looked back at the young man. Track pants. High-vis vest. An old Nokia in his hand. A creature with scales down its back and a long flicking tail, rising in curls up one side of his neck.

---

1   The Expressway is being built by a group called the Alliance. The group is made up of the New Zealand Transport Agency, Fletcher Construction, Beca Planning and Infrastructure and Higgins Group, supported by Goodmans Contractors, Incite and Boffa Miskell.

2   In other parts of the country a taniwha has been known to hold a wife captive by tying a rope around her, so that she can work, but not run away. At the time when I met the young man, I did not know there could be a connection between taniwha and ropes.

In this moment the idea arrived that a [taniwha] might be connected to this man and to this place. The [taniwha] I detected was made of, or lives in, water, had been disturbed by the attempts to drain the swamp, and would, in the end, be stronger than the road. It was a whole story. To say this surprised me is an understatement. The young man had not, at this point, even mentioned the swamp.

•

'It's such a big thing,' I said [the Expressway]. 'And it changes so fast.'

'Yeah,' he said.

'What's the Alliance like to work for?' I asked.

'It's all right, I suppose,' he said. 'We work ten-hour days. People come along all the time and some of them come onto the site yelling that it's wrong and we shouldn't be building it,' he said. 'And cursing, too.[3] I don't argue,' he said. 'We have to keep good relations with the public. And anyway, if one of them made a complaint over there at the office, they'd soon work out who it was . . . '

I made a motherly noise.

'I understand how they feel, anyway, the ones that are against it. I'd feel the same if it was me,' he continued. 'I feel like telling them it's nothing to do with me. It's coming from way up high. The other day we had the big boss here and he was telling us that he has a boss and his boss has a boss, and we just have to do our job.'

I made a bread-on-the-table noise.

'I'm just a very unimportant man,' the young man said. 'I support myself and my partner and our baby. We moved down from Hawke's Bay for this job.'

---

3   That was his word, cursing.

'The other day,' he said, 'a dude here said that this road had been in the pipeline for thirty years. They should have known it was coming.'

I offered the idea that in my time there had been a local road marked on council maps but not an Expressway.

'Anyway, they started on Transmission Gully last week,' he said. 'There needs to be another way out of Wellington. It only takes one slip and the coastal highway is closed. My partner and I moved here last year just when we had those earthquakes and we thought there definitely needs to be another way to get out of Wellington.'

I nodded. Anyone who lives here would nod at this.

'See those two hills there?' The man pointed. 'That's where the Transmission Gully Road will go. They're using yellow rock over there to push down and force out the water,' he said, pointing to the south side of Poplar Road.[4] 'It used to be a swamp, 'he said. 'All marshy.'

'Yes,' I said. In my time there had been puddles, pūkeko, swirls of mist on winter mornings, ragged horses and bright yellow gorse at this corner.

'I worked over there for months and I asked what they are doing. They told me they take all the peat away and then they put the yellow rock down and the theory is that the yellow rock presses down and any water left down there is squished out the sides. And then these surveyor guys come and they put pipes underneath and they can see if the water is being squished down and out to the side like it is supposed to.'

'And is it?' I asked.

---

4   Once I saw a pūkeko standing vigil beside its dead mate, right where he was pointing.

'I don't know,' he said.

At this time construction of the Expressway had been underway for about nine months.

•

Nine months later, things are very different down at the intersection of State Highway 1 and Poplar Avenue. The Expressway is so big and so straight that you can see it from space. Also from the hill above the Nikau Reserve. Raised above the surrounding land, the road stretches north from Poplar Avenue towards the next site headquarters at Kāpiti Road, the Waikanae River, Otaihanga, and from there towards its final destination, Peka Peka. From a distance the Expressway looks timeless and a little military, which led me to speculate on Twitter about the involvement of reincarnated Romans.

The Expressway isn't a black road yet. It still shows its yellow rock foundation, but already it is metres and metres higher than Poplar Avenue or State Highway 1. I have not heard anyone talking about this, but as the yellow road grows higher and longer, the quarry hole in the side of the hill behind Paraparaumu, where the yellow rock comes from, is growing wider and deeper. The concrete Virgin Mary who used to sit high above Paraparaumu has not shifted, but somehow, with this huge hole beside her, she looks lower now.

Up on top of the yellow road, the men are as small as Lego men and their enormous machines look as if they would be good in a sandpit. One day I tweeted that the men washing the machines were children playing under a hose.

The contractors have dug out dark and boggy peat, made piles of it and separate piles of the logs submerged in the peat. They have even given some of the peat away. We have a few sacks full now, in the garden, where we grow broad beans. There was so much peat piled up that even with the whole neighbourhood there, taking the peat away in trailers, only a symbolic amount was moved.

In a poem I have described the peat as breathing.

At Poplar Avenue itself, the pillars that will hold up a bridge are in place now. I have described these pillars as hands opening wide in the shape of a bowl, waiting to receive some gift.

Beside the yellow Expressway is the haul road.[5] Sometimes the road-builders hang festive red flags over the haul road. For them the red flags are a height warning. For me, one day they were tatty flags put out by a visiting circus, and on another day they were echoes of a Russian submarine putting on the Ritz in the harbour at Vladivostok. Since the day the [taniwha] came into my mind I have joked on Twitter about the Expressway perhaps two hundred times.

At some point I noticed that I keep trying to see the Expressway as something else. I left this verb in the present tense, because even today I noticed some sacking draped over a bridge pillar and felt an urge to make it into something else. This compulsion is a very interesting situation. I have asked myself whether it happens because I am not the right sort of writer to write about a road, being more a psychologist than an engineer. Or whether the only way I could write about the sheer massiveness and imposition of the road is to carve off little pieces of it and turn each of those into a joke.

Over these last months I've found myself with a recurrent awareness of the road as an exoskeleton, expanding across the sand and the wetlands, ready to join up. The word 'awareness' is a pale version of the experience I am trying to describe here. I am talking about feeling the rigidity of the road spreading over the land as if it was steel spreading across my own skin. Something about the rigidity of all this concrete, compared with the soggy peat, made me understand, on that September day in 2014, that the road and the water in the peat are enemies. First I heard from the young man that the road-builders saw the watery peat as an enemy.

---

5   A haul road is the road you build to carry the materials and men you need to build a road.

Then suddenly it seemed possible that the water and the peat might see the concrete as an enemy.

It's still quite a jump from 'enemies' to a [taniwha]. More than likely I saw a 'false' or metaphorical taniwha. A taniwha does not have to be a lizard, by the way. It can also take the shape of a log.

Commentaries on 'The [taniwha] of Poplar Avenue'

1

In the winter of 1995, my partner and I met a Māori colleague in the supermarket. We had one of those 'What are you guys doing in the weekend?' conversations. I don't remember what she said she was doing but we said we were heading 'up the mountain' for some skiing.[6] We must have also said that we were looking forward to seeing the mountain, because she said something like 'I hope the mountain wants to see *you*'. My head spun when she said this and I thought about her comment for a long time. But then I half-forgot it for nearly 20 years.

I don't know how other people's ideas arrive. Mine creep in. Then they creep forward, an inch or two at a time while my back is turned, a bit like the game of Statues. Often, when I finally discover that a new idea has arrived, I see that it has already appeared several times before. I see this most clearly in my writing,

---

6   That is how we spoke of Mt Ruapehu.

because the texts are such a clear record of what I have been thinking about. It may seem odd that an idea could be known but not known, remembered and half-forgotten, found, lost and then re-found, but that is how it works.

2

In November 2014 at the *Placing the Personal Essay Colloquium* at Massey University Wellington, I heard the words 'the agency of place'. I had probably heard these words before but I hadn't *really* heard them (see above).

In the case of 'the agency of place', there were many events that I can look back on now and recognise as moments when it became more and more likely that I would think that a magical creature capable of smashing the MacKays to Peka Peka Expressway with one flick of its tail might rise up out of wetlands near the intersection of Poplar Avenue and State Highway.

One such moment was the film *Voices of the Land: Ngā Reo o te Whenua*, which I saw in July 2014. Water crashed, flax rattled and the wind blew flutey notes. Previously I had listened to these noises and found pleasure in them. After the film I listened for these voices.

3

Edvard Munch's painting 'The Scream' is not a representation of a man screaming into the fjord, but is in fact, itself a scream,' says Goldfarb in the introduction to Bruno Schulz's *The Street of Crocodiles and Other Stories*.[7] Goldfarb quotes Witkacy Witkiewicz's view that poetry, painting and drama could represent 'the metaphysical feeling of the strangeness of existence', but prose 'could only represent the experience of the individual in the face of this [feeling]'. According to Witkiewicz, Bruno Schulz's prose was the one exception to this rule.

---

7   David A Goldfarb, Introduction, *The Street of Crocodiles and other stories*, by Bruno Schulz, trans Celina Wieniewska (Penguin: New York, 2008), xv.

4

Bruno Schulz is not much discussed in New Zealand. I wish he were discussed more.

5

Back in 1995 I used to walk along the banks of the Manawatu River almost every day. After a lot of rain, the water level between the banks would rise, as everyone expects with rivers. But water also travelled through and across flat land and appeared, a kilometre or two away, in our backyard.

Around that time I had been reading a lot about the Golem of Prague. Pudgy clay could be shaped into a man. Magic words would bring him to life. He could do things ordinary men could not. One day, as I was walking by the Manawatu River, I smelled cold river clay and kawakawa leaves and realised that we could make him here, in Aotearoa, if we needed him badly enough.

6

Some people think that creative texts and commentary, when placed side by side, compete for air. When I was discussing the idea of a story and a commentary with another writer, she said, as a sort of sympathetic murmur, that one of the two texts would probably become stronger than the other. I think she meant that when that happened, I should abort the weaker twin.

7

In the case of my twins, the [taniwha] story began as a poem in September 2014 and the commentaries began in December 2014. In between, I attended the colloquium and noticed that the story already knew something about 'the agency of place'. This is an example of the phenomenon I described in (1). From December on, the commentaries suggested further developments of the story and vice versa. How could one be a favourite?

8

Karl Ove Knausgaard and his wife Linda are seated in a grubby café, not looking at each other. On the table is a large plate of soggy-looking chips. If we are to believe what he says, Knausgaard himself is not a fan of 'the novel' as a form, preferring to hear from people writing about their own lives, rather than hear stories that are couched as 'made up'.

The argument Knausgaard is making seems to me to justify this rather substantial paragraph.

> The only genres I saw value in, which conferred meaning, were diaries and essays, the types of literature that did not deal with narrative, that were not about anything, but just consisted of a voice, the voice of your personality, a life, a face, a gaze you could meet. What is a work of art if not the gaze of another person? Not directed above us, nor beneath us, but at the same height as our own gaze. Art cannot be experienced collectively, nothing can, art is something you are alone with. You meet its gaze alone.[8]

9

A human voice begins with a beating heart. It moves as air through open pipes, past gateways and is expelled as ideas. After that expulsion, the ideas have been said and cannot be unsaid.

I listen to human voices out of respect for the raw arrogance, the transience, the vulnerability, the ridiculousness, the singularity and the humility of a voice. Speech breaks my heart.

I listen out of nosiness too. I want to find out what each person knows. I am equally happy to hear voices from a soap opera, a novel, a piece of graffiti, a sitcom, gossip or a piece of scholarship. My ability to understand what voices say varies. Say, for example, I listened to flax or to the sea. What could I ever make of that voice? So many things are in the way.

---

8   Karl Ove Knausgaard, *A Man in Love*, trans Don Bartlett (London: Harvill Secker, 2013), 496–7.

10

Back in the late 1970s I was trained in the science of observing others. Only actions counted. Words were seen as murky, unreliable, shifty characters and were to be discounted.

11

Even though we tried to reduce our personal impositions, there was acknowledged to be a certain frisson caused by the presence of a psychologist in someone's living room.

This was called 'reactivity' and could be reduced if the psychologist kept very still and stayed a long time. Helen Macdonald, beginning to train a goshawk, says 'you must learn to become invisible'. 'I don't look at her. I mustn't. What I am doing is concentrating very hard on the process of *not being there*,'[9] she says. The similarity to my own experiences in various living rooms is striking.

12

I was trained never to use the first person pronoun when I wrote about what I saw. There was a real knack to writing without letting on that you saw something or that you were the writer. The difficulty was trebled when it came to stating an opinion. The writing itself tended to long sentences and was very dull to read, although there was also a pleasant sense of discipline and self-denial in the reading experience. At the time, of course, I was an 'insider' reader of these texts, and all the hints, allusions and nuances reminded me of that. This knowledge was a form of pleasure too.

13

Behind all this passive construction and recursion there was a strange sense of an unnamed powerful being lurking somewhere back at the beginning of these arguments. At one time I thought that being was my thesis supervisor, and then

---

9   Helen Macdonald, *H is for Hawk* (Jonathan Cape: London, 2014), 67.

later, that it was B.F. Skinner, or three professors in Kansas named Baer, Wolf and Risley. Quite a lot later, in the early 1990s, while studying in Canada, the thought came to me that perhaps I, containing my world, was the one behind all the arguments. With that, I threw away the clipboard and the idea of objectivity and put my faith in the zeitgeist.

14

I believe that the zeitgeist, the place and time and the prevailing anxieties and certainties of the clan, pass through the placenta as freely as nutrients and alcohol, and are therefore present in a child at birth. Furthermore, I believe that this zeitgeist cannot be removed. I think it can be obscured by other later sediments, remain uncontested or be fought against. I think it can be somewhat attenuated by keeping company with different essences. But, overall, and finally, I think of the place and time of one's birth act like anchovies in a sauce; not discernible as themselves but present as a salty essence, deep and influential.

15

I was born in Hāwera, New Zealand, in 1954, to Pākehā parents with white-collar jobs. Sometimes there was an unexplained sound like ice creaking. I used to look at the word 'Hāwera' and think it was strange. Now I know the name commemorates a battle and is made up of two words; 'ha', meaning 'breath', and 'wera', meaning 'fire'. The name of the town wasn't English and neither were we, as it turned out.

Today, in Raumati, I am listening to the wind that roars around my house like a bellows, trying to understand what the northwest wind means. Rain falls up in the hills and water runs down towards the coast. Pūkeko are very territorial. These are things I know. Opinions differ on whether the Golem of Prague was a shapeless mass or a strong man without a soul, and perhaps, having been brought to life, he went mad and ran amok, but whether literal or symbolic, he made the people feel safer. That is the point.

Lynn Jenner is the author of a poetry collection, *Dear Sweet Harry*, which won the NZSA Jessie Mackay Award for Best First Book of Poetry 2011, and *Lost and Gone Away* (2015). She writes:

I live in the discipline of creative writing. Lots of different tribes live in here, and I am grateful that the mongrel tribe to which I belong has a place inside the wall. I think perhaps our numbers are growing.

My aim is to make the form, structure, appearance and apparatus of my texts into another full version of the content. I think of this primarily as an aesthetic activity, a little like sculpture. In my mind I am carving shapes out of words and white space to make a thing. For me questions of genre and how we think about text are as (small p) political as what the words say, although I realise others may not see it this way. I am very interested to hear the voices from across disciplinary borders in this book. Tuning in to voices from across borders helps with most things.

I am currently researching the relationships between critical and creative components of a PhD in creative writing, so I have been listening to lots of opinions about how this can work. That is yet another layer of what is behind the story of the [taniwha].

By Your Place in the World, I Will Know Who You Are

Tina Makereti

Last year I attended a hui for a new job and was among a group of people who were, for the most part, unfamiliar. I knew a handful of attendees, so in one of the breaks I greeted an old acquaintance, and she introduced me to the other people in her group.

She said something like 'Tina is a writer' by way of introduction.

'Oh?' said one of her group, then she looked at me intently, curiously and without recognition. 'Where are you from?'

At this point I did what I always do when faced with this question. I stumbled and stuttered, and muttered something about being from all over the place, but currently, up the coast.

'The East Coast?' she asked, her interest piqued.

'Uh no, Kāpiti Coast,' and stumbled around further, trying to find purchase in this exchange of niceties that is quintessentially Māori.

What I like about this encounter, despite my discomfort, was that the woman enquiring of my origins was blond and had Pākehā features. I had thought she was Pākehā, and perhaps she was, but when she spoke, her intonation and her question immediately revealed something about her cultural origins or associations. Her expression was one I have only encountered from Māori seeking to make connections. And her question meant: 'I will be able to place you if I know where you're from. By your place in the world, I will know who you are.'

As soon as this happened, I felt culturally inadequate, but that had nothing to do with skin or features or any outward expressions of identity. It was about knowing your place in the world.

Each time I encounter this question, I feel like I fail a small test, no matter how hard I work to come to terms with the lack of precision and definition in my answer.

Sometimes writing a personal essay feels like a constant argument about place— the place I belong, how I place myself, my place between cultures—a constant wrangling between two sides that at its simplest is embodied by my Māori and Pākehā parentages. The marriage between my Pākehā father and Māori mother didn't work, and they separated when I was still a toddler. My sister and I were brought up by our father. It's not important to go into the details of that, suffice to say I still remember the exact moment when, as a teenager, I began to see my parents' relationship as a microcosm of the historical relationship between Pākehā and Māori. This analogy was of some use to a confused young woman, although time and maturity eventually caused me to view my parents, and history, as more complex creatures. However the outcome of all of this was something that doesn't make much sense, something paradoxical if you will—a Māori who doesn't come from any place in particular. Tūrangawaewae or papakāinga are widely held by Māori and Pākehā as defining features in placing who Māori are.[1] As Indigenous peoples, as Treaty partners, as tangata whenua, knowledge of and relationship to ancestral land is paramount in explaining and maintaining not just personal but political and economic claims to tino rangatiratanga, or sovereign status. Knowing where you come from really matters.

But if I am asked where I come from, I can't give a direct or single answer. This is particularly problematic when meeting other Māori, for whom it is more common and polite to ask where you're from than who you are. Not only was I brought up without any knowledge of my papakāinga, but we also moved places every year or two. I do not have a 'hometown', even in the Pākehā sense.

This void or absence should not be confused with not having any relationship to homeplaces. I do have multiple papakāinga; that is, I have several mountains, waters, lands and marae that I connect to via whakapapa or genealogical and familial links. These are my places to stand, and I can go to any of them at any time and find myself 'home'. I don't mean some ephemeral, non-experiential sense of home; I mean that they quite literally, physically embody home spaces for me. One summer several years ago I was doing novel research in Waikawa Bay, Picton. I hoped to find evidence of stories I had heard about my ancestry that had inspired the fiction. Waikawa is my grandfather's marae and therefore very much mine, but I had not been there for approximately a decade and we knew few people who still lived in the area. My first stop was the urupā where I could greet my ancestors and seek the ones related to my story.[2] It is an extraordinary place at the height of summer, high on a hill above the Sounds, and I always feel as though the tupuna get a pretty nice view to watch over for all of eternity. I took my children exploring with me and told them what I could of our connections, and as we were leaving we visited a second spot with additional graves. Here, an aunty took me in hand. Who were my people? she asked.

---

1   Often translated, respectively as 'place to stand' and 'homeplace', also known as haukāinga.
2   Urupā translates to cemetery.

I told her my grandfather's name. Oh, you're one of ours. Are you coming to the marae? There's a tangi, one of your relations. Come have a kai. Do you have somewhere to stay?

And so, even though I hadn't told anyone we were coming, even though I wouldn't have known who to tell we were coming, there we were, home, and not one person looked at me like I was a stranger, even though I kind of was. I was theirs, they were mine—that was my place. It is possible for me to do that on six marae, maybe more. Nothing I write in this essay and none of my discomfort refutes the fact that they are inexorably *my places*. But I wasn't brought up near them. I did not spend my childhood playing around their marae ātea, or sleepily looking up at the rafters of the whare while hui went on for days. Most Māori identify more strongly with one or two places, one or two iwi. Mother and father. Even if we leave out the fractured beginnings and the Pākehā upbringing, I have trouble claiming just one or two of these marae as my main places. Where are you from? For me, the answer is at least a paragraph, if not a page. Never a sentence.

It feels somewhat ridiculous to be concerned about this—six marae, maybe more? Surely I am drowning in cultural riches. But the ahi kā, also known as 'keeping the home fires burning', is a tikanga that can't be discounted. If I don't live by these marae, if I don't contribute to them regularly, if the people there don't see my face each month, or even year, how can I maintain my place there? I'm a townie. I live where I hope to make a good life for my children. I choose to expend my cultural energy in writing and urban cultural activity, for the most part. I operate in the wider world as Māori even though I don't always know how to 'be' Māori when Māori are by definition tribal. For example, I can't choose between my western or central dialect: should I say 'whakapapa' or 'w_akapapa'? There is whakamā, which translates as something like shame or embarrassment, in all of this.

Put simply, there is an expectation that Māori know where they come from, yet I write as a Māori who doesn't have grounding in one place, one tribe, or one

169

culture, but who is still Māori. I am Pākehā too. I am not part-Māori and part-Pākehā; I am *both* Māori and Pākehā.

One great solace and encouragement is that while the specificities of this story are uniquely mine, the outcome is not—we, whatever we are, are everywhere. There are labels—variations on hybrid, urban Māori, ngā awarua. There's even a movement to reclaim the title 'half-caste'. It really shouldn't be such a big deal anymore, except I still can't answer a simple question, 'Where are you from?' and I still meet young people who are deeply conflicted, even ashamed, about their multiple heritages.

I often think of writing in terms of paradox.

How can two seemingly opposite ideas exist in the same place?

Do they actually exist in the same place? Are they actually opposites? How can someone be from more than one place and more than one or two or five peoples?

The place I write from comprises two opposite and conflicting ideas: one, that I absolutely belong to multiple places in Aotearoa, that I have inalienable rights to those places as tangata whenua; and two, that until I was almost an adult, there was a void in my life where papakāinga or homeplaces should have been. A void which also should have been occupied by cultural and familial knowledge, and which is no longer unusual among either Māori or Pākehā. This paradoxical place is extraordinarily powerful to write from: teetering on the edge of the void, buoyed constantly by absolute belonging and knowledge subsequently gained as an adult. It is the pain and loss and discomfort of the void thrown up against the wealth of what I now know that informs what I do. It's something I'm grateful for every time I write, because writing is itself an enactment of that very same tension: of what we don't understand, what we yearn for, what we seek, and what we know utterly, at the level of bones.

I have written about Māori versus European conceptions of the universe, Pākehā-Māori ancestors from the 19th century (the original hybrids) and about loving museums and being confused about their history of containing and misrepresenting, even maiming their collections, including people. I've written about how crucial it is to use Māori words in English-language stories, the strange rightness of a carved tauihu in a European museum, the feeling I sometimes have that ghosts might linger in my writing, or maybe that is just a way to explain things. In each of these essays, there is a tension from the first line—this is how I know I should keep writing. Even now I feel it, the impossibility of making what I'm trying to say clear, transparent, sensible, straightforward. It isn't. Māori and European systems of understanding the universe are almost identical, except in the ways they are not. Pākehā-Māori were Europeans who assimilated themselves into Māori culture by choice and desire, except they were still Pākehā. A carving from a 19th-century waka should not belong in a museum in Frankfurt, except that somehow it does.

The essay is the perfect site to explore paradoxical questions because an essay is supposed to be nonfiction, which means it is supposed to be about a knowable truth. And yet the essays I enjoy circle around the unknowable, constantly trying to place a finger on what something is, constantly searching for answers to questions the writer knows are, at some level, unanswerable. Fiction does this too, but fiction has permission to do anything it wants. Don't know who you are? Make something up! With nonfiction there is a tension already on the page from the moment we touch pen to page or fingers to keyboard. The tension comes from nonfiction's imperative to write something true when we don't even know if that's possible. Essays ask us to achieve the unattainable, like being multiple things and coming from multiple places all at once. How do I understand the complexities of a simple encounter like the one at that work hui, with all its layers of culture and nuance, differing understandings about the significance of not just physical but cultural place, and appearance? I write a personal essay, though I'm not sure I will find my way to any particular answer by the end of it.

I love the challenge and the impossibility of the form. I can gather evidence. I can draw pictures, design diagrams and problem-solve. I can quote the greats.

Occasionally, I can capture a reflection, sample soil or draw blood. I might even get satisfaction from evoking a sense of how I understand the world, but what I can't do is present what I have written as fact. The Way Things Are is changeable, difficult to corral into tidy yards. Things like place and identity can't be captured, but fleeting glimpses of them can be. I struggle with those personal pronouns at the centre of the personal essay—the great 'I' and 'me'. But what I'm really talking about—by extension, I hope—is us. How does it work for any of us? What does *tangata whenua* mean in this moment?[3] Suffice to say that the essay is a place where we can make, as Albert Wendt pointed out in his iconic 1976 essay 'Towards a New Oceania', our individual journeys into the Void, where we can explain us to ourselves. I have used the essay as a site to make ancestral journeys, and these explorations have only complicated my understandings of where I come from, rather than simplified them. There has been no single path, no single people, no single place that takes precedence in these stories. But knowing the stories, getting closer to the heart of the contradictions, has taken away some of the whakamā. I can only view the complexity of what the tupuna have left behind as a gift, a place that offers comfort even where it does not provide certainty.

Postscript

A new question arises now, one I had not understood to ask when I first wrote this essay: What does *mana whenua* mean in this moment?[3] A week after submitting this essay we returned to Waikawa for a long weekend with my

---

3 In the process of discussing this essay, as well as her own, with editor Ingrid Horrocks, I came to understand what mana whenua means as distinct from tangata whenua. Mana whenua refers to the people with ancestral rights (mana) in the actual region being referred to; tangata whenua refers to all 'people of the land' or Māori, wherever they live. Therefore I can live in Wellington as tangata whenua but I am not mana whenua. In Picton, I am mana whenua. It seems extraordinary to me that I had not grasped this concept fully before writing this essay, which has become, due to the trip to Picton, an experiential enactment of the various concepts described herein.

family-in-law. The trip had been planned, serendipitously enough, by a sister-in-law who knew nothing of my connections there. I knew we would be close to my people. In fact our cottage was nestled under the hill where my ancestors rest. We went to see them. We passed the marae each day. In the new whale centre and the old museum my great-great-great-grandparents were alive in black and white stills.

I can't remember who said it first. *We could live here*. We *should* live here. Look at the hills. Look at the sea.

It had not seemed like a possibility before. Imagine living in a place where the tupuna are everywhere, we said. Making a real contribution to the marae. Imagine how it would feel to have that much sureness when your feet touch the earth. I could see that one day I may be that person. The young ones will come to visit from the city and think there's no way they could live in this small nowhere town no matter how beautiful it is. They probably won't ever live near one of their marae. This is what I thought. But no matter how much you and your whakapapa wander, the homeplace calls.

Tina Makereti writes essays, novels and short stories. Her novel, *Where the Rēkohu Bone Sings* (Vintage, 2014), won the 2014 Ngā Kupu Ora Aotearoa Māori Book Award for Fiction and was longlisted for the IMPAC Dublin Literary Award 2015. Her short story collection, *Once Upon a Time in Aotearoa*, also won Ngā Kupu Ora's fiction prize in 2011. In 2009 she was the recipient of the Royal Society of New Zealand Manhire Prize for Creative Science Writing (nonfiction) and the Pikihuia Award for Best Short Story Written in English. Tina is Curator Māori for Museums Wellington and also convenes a Māori and Pasifika Creative Writing Workshop at Victoria University. She is of Te Āti Awa, Ngāti Tūwharetoa, Ngāti Rangatahi, Pākehā and, according to family stories, Moriori descent. www.tinamakereti.com

The meshing of thought and world

A Real Piece: Available Globally via PostShop, REAL Aotearoa, 0800NZstamps

Ian Wedde

An autoethnographic essay into the shifty and shifting place of the real on location and on set, constructed in the mind of an adult with the help of a five-year-old child by a New Zealand Post/MGM marketing campaign.

Nostalgic nationalism

While not wanting to re-enter 'Middle-earth', a place that has had most of its discursive oxygen sucked out, I'm going to focus on my encounter with an item of merchandise marketing by New Zealand Post that—like it or not—will return me to that place whose reality is at once jammed with contesting narratives, and strangely hollow.

   This involves the ordinary activity of a morning walk to the post office and then on to a café for a cup of coffee. It's something I do most days, usually with my wife Donna. A lot of people do the same, and we greet some of them, but only occasionally as close friends. As an exercise in autoethnography research it's got to be a low-yield option—a somewhat shallow social regime.

But there are various markers along the way that could at a pinch be mined. There's a large Australian eucalypt whose roots are pushing up the pavement just past our place, and an abundant frangipani tree a bit further up the road. The botanical topography of the inner city and its traces of Australian-Irish and Pacific working-class cultures might be a research option. This could inaugurate a novel-of-ideas—an essay—about the dynastic interrelationships of an Irish-Australian and a Pacific Island family as the working class suburb of Ponsonby underwent its process of *embourgeoisement* and Ponsonby Road became chic. It wasn't chic when I lived here as a student in the 1960s, so there's also a subject-position reserved for me in this story.

The morning traffic along the feeder link to the harbour bridge provides a slow-moving portrait gallery of commuter activity and emotion. This could become a fixed-viewpoint camera video essay in which a passing parade of cellphone-checking, nose-picking, hair-fixing, and child-pacifying is observed without comment. Much could be made of the morning's joggers; their preferences for black sportswear, the proportion of them who have small dogs running alongside and their disproportionate gender weighting towards women. And so on. But usually, I walk along this familiar route after a short morning stint clearing emails and stuff, my thoughts elsewhere, immersed in rather than observant of what's around me.

This is an urban narrative, but because the city of its location—Auckland—is a small one, it retains vestiges of small-town social and cultural geography. Its intimacy is that of small crowd space rather than big crowd crush. The exuberant woman who runs the post-office box service is often sitting outside by the back entrance we use, having a smoke and a cup of tea, and she'll greet us cheerfully with a 'Morning, darlings!' It's a neighbourly atmosphere. The owner of the café we go to after clearing the mail has a daughter living in Melbourne, where my son Jack also lives—our kids are friends. Nonetheless, there's a perceptible tension between the neighbourhood and the global. Some of the regulars at the café, including my wife Donna, work in film and television and are involved with international contacts on a regular basis. Unless they're travelling, their small place intersects with big place via Skype calls and the like. These relationships are articulated virtually, for the most part, along a north–south axis governed by international time and season zones, as a result of which morning talks to evening, winter to summer, and so on. No doubt there are diurnal and seasonal fluctuations of emotion and thought along this axis—gloomy end-of-winter days talking to cheerful summer mornings, and so forth.

Then there are young tourists from large European, Asian and American cities who stay at the Brown Kiwi backpackers just down the road and enter the café as visitors from big to small. This relationship is articulated physically—in fact, one often hears comments about how lovely it is to be really *in* an uncrowded place with a beautiful unspoiled landscape. This is a mindset that often turns out to have been pre-programmed by the international phenomenon of Middle-earth as promoted by Peter Jackson's *Hobbit* movies. The congested traffic around the café in Three Lamps must disappoint many of these optimists, and I sometimes hear them discussing this.

These are familiar and even banal terms of engagement, haunted by all-too-familiar ghosts of nationalist and/or nostalgic models.

So, one morning I enter the post office in my usual low-attention state and there see a poster inviting me to 'Get a real piece of Middle-earth'. At this point, whether I like it or not, I know that when I get to the café I'm going to write this sentence down in my notebook, and that it will, sooner or later, inaugurate some thinking and writing—an *essay*—that will fold the narrative of my routine together with a list of paradoxical challenges thrown at me by the post-office poster; and that this will happen despite my disinclination to be drawn into an already exhausted discussion about whether 'distance looks our way' or not.

It's just as likely that what I've jotted down in my notebook will make its way into an essay—that is, the product of some thinking and writing—in the form of a novel, or even a poem. I don't know where this little shock of *noticing* will end up, and I don't really care. The notebook I carry around with me is full of stuff whose final destination is often uncertain or unknown. What's important is that I've *noticed*, that my mind has been happily provoked into thought, that my heart is beating a little faster and that all at once the world seems to be more interesting than it was.

In effect, research involving this folding-together of a personal narrative and a thought-provoking issue has been underway for some time, since its basic field-work plan is my regular morning excursion to the post office and across the street to the café. What's now changed is the fact that the accumulated information of this daily routine has been charged with a purpose because of the poster in the post office. In Geertzian terms, I can now begin to unpack an accumulated 'thick description' of the event for material to 'include in the consultable record'. I can begin to move from inscription to specification, if I want to. And in fact, even without wanting to programme what I might do in the form of a Geertzian autoethnography, I'm pretty much doing so involuntarily.

I'm doing this not just by default, but because I'm a writer, and am therefore the kind of reader who is excited not just by the content of what I read, but by what I might learn from its techniques. Over the years I've read a fair bit of ethnographic literature, and have recently reread the 2000 edition of Clifford Geertz's 1960s essays, which were mind-changing for me when I first encountered them in the 1970s. The personal essay, here, is not simply an effect that is somehow extruded by the pressure of my subject position within the observed event. It is also a narrative that has another writer's presence at its shoulder or, indeed, 'in mind'. In Georges Poulet's terms, which were roughly contemporaneous with those of Geertz, I find myself in the uncanny situation of thinking another's thoughts. So from quite early in this piece, I encountered Clifford Geertz and Georges Poulet in conversation with the first-person me, whose viewpoint directed the narrative, but whose consciousness has been strategically occupied by the thinking of others—an occupation, it has to be added, that has remained provisional, indeed *mobile*, through the 40 years since my first encounter with these writers.

Mobility, migration and place

We are beginning to circle around another of the themes with which this collection is concerned—'How might we talk about the relationships between mobility, migration and place?' Parking, for the time being, the mobility of thoughts jostling in our minds over time, and the mobility of those jostled-in minds in and out of different locations and conditions, this theme is most often deployed around discussions—or stories—of belonging (or not), of 'settling' or 'unsettling', of the problematic, paradoxical nature of home; and will have used and often worn out a vocabulary struggling to be at once forensic and descriptive, for example 'diasporic'.

The discussion has found a productive local terminology in what the late Geoff Park characterised as a disjunction between European concepts of landscape shaped by viewing, and Māori concepts of whenua shaped by embodiment. This language has had useful counterparts elsewhere, for example in the frequent use of the word 'situated' by both James Clifford and Donna Haraway in the United States, signalling the need for ethnographic work of whatever kind to proceed from an acute awareness of context and conditions and, therefore, of their shifts and shiftinesses.

But I'd like to tackle this theme from a different perspective, albeit one that requires the point of view to be *situated*, to be reflexively aware of how it's placed. Our deepest (thickest) awareness of the mental and spatial mobility of thought—of how our own thoughts and those of others are constantly migrating, visiting, conversing to and fro across borders—will usually derive from our adult relationships (if we are adults). Such relationships will be diasporic, or distanced, only to the extent that their cultural contexts are unsettling. If we are curious about (rather than merely tolerant of) difference we will welcome and even seek out such diasporic unsettlings. They are what we expect of grown-up conversation. But there are other opportunities close to home, situated or embodied in ways we too easily take for granted and therefore overlook.

A couple of days ago Donna came home from visiting our five-year-old granddaughter Bella, to whom she'd delivered a present from her great-grandparents. The present was a blond-haired doll. Bella, whose part-Samoan parentage has given her a head of lush black curls, was pleased with the doll, but wanted to know where she was from. Fearing that Bella might be anxious about her own identity in relation to the blond doll's, Donna began a conversation about Bella's question, 'Where are you from?' As it turned out, Bella was asking what movie or TV show the doll was from. Was she a Princess Merida, a Cinderella, an Aurora, a Rapunzel or—best of all, just then—an Elsa, the snow queen of the Disney animated feature *Frozen*? Identity is artefactual, but the artefact will come to life through imaginative play that is informed by the character's backstory. The blond doll will enter Bella's life because her story already has. Bella will put her in play with other toys whose stories she also knows. Then she will mash the stories up and make new identities for the dolls, because that's the most fun thing to do. This mash-up will essay or try out personality; it will be a personal essay about the relationships between mobility, migration and place—including the 'place' of the movies. More on this place soon.

Personal and cultural memory

Bella's mash-up may also essay and be an essay about personal and cultural memory. However, I'd like to tackle this issue by means of yet another anecdote. I have a twin brother, Dave, who is blessed with an exceptional memory and tremendous equanimity. My memory is unreliable, and I'm given to melodrama. The collective family memory—a cultural memory—has bequeathed both of us a story about the time when, as infants just getting our first teeth, we were taken for a walk in our double pram by our grandmother, Aggie Horne. All at once, so the family memory asserts, the normally happy Dave began to shriek. Nana Horne assumed it was me, but as it turned out it was Dave who was screaming. The reason was that we'd managed to swap thumbs to suck, and I was sucking his—but had also begun to gnash it with a sharp new tooth.

The family liked this story because, over the years, it consolidated and transmitted their sense of how my devious character was shaping up. But my brother is quite sure that the biting was being done by him, that it was me who was shrieking, and that Aggie got it wrong. But since neither of us can in fact remember what happened, we have only the family's cultural memory to go by, and that was the product of much hilarious repetition of Aggie Horne's eye-witness account. But since all members of the family who might be consulted about this eye-witness account (or essay) have been dead for many years, we are left with a space of uncertainty between the realist Dave's account and that of his fantasist twin. Out of this space a number of potential narrative threads emerge—for example, does either of us accurately remember how the family story went when we first heard it at an age we could retain it? Did I in effect overwrite the family's version because, back then, I wanted to be the biter? Or was Nana Horne wrong about the biter, but allowed herself to be persuaded that I was he because that fitted her uneasy sense of how the infant Ian was developing?

We will never know. What matters, in terms of the personal essay, is that this space of narrative unreliability is probably its greatest asset, and is what by and large distinguishes its kind of epistemology from that of the academic essay, reliant as that usually is on reductive and contestable measures of truth, and on a watchful perimeter of scrupulous citation. The personal essay's narrative unreliability is rich in many ways, but perhaps richest in the destabilising effects it has on first-person presence and on the ambiguities that consequently attend the question of who, exactly, is situated, exactly, where? Yes, I can be clear and forthright about the ways in which I'm embedded—situated—in this or that narrative. But the pleasure this presence might generate in readers is about imaginative truth-values, about play and about orders of reality that are multi-perspectival, digressive and contradictory. Bella knows this, and enjoys inventing and then subverting identities when we play.

The ironic or self-reflexive *style indirect libre* as deployed by Flaubert in *Madame Bovary* is perhaps the most obvious model of what this parsing of first and third person (plus author) presences can accomplish—and *Madame Bovary* has always seemed to me to be an *essay*, an ethnography, about the unstable values of bourgeois reality and of subject positions within that reality; and to be an essay not rather than, but because it is also, a novel. The personal essay's ontology may disclose impeccably observed correspondences between words and facts—but we encounter these truths through subjectivities that invite us to play with the essay's construction of reality. The model is less one of a helpful, perhaps patronising, arms-length hermeneutics, more one of a deliberately unhelpful seduction, an invitation to get situated by joining in a game whose rules are contingent on us agreeing to play.

'A real piece'

Finally, back to the poster in the Ponsonby post office that got me started on this line of enquiry.

The poster promises us 'a real piece of Middle-earth', but since we know that Middle-earth doesn't really exist, the poster seems to be in flagrant breach of advertising standards. However, as my granddaughter Bella knows, the answer in respect of where the 'real piece' comes from, is: from a movie, stupid. But how, then, can the 'piece' be 'real' in a material sense? The answer is in the small print. The exculpatory text reads . . . contains real wood from the Hobbiton movie set'.

Harking back for a moment to an ontology that may 'disclose impeccably observed correspondences between words and facts', we can say with confidence that the 'real wood' referred to in the New Zealand Post media small print does, physically, exist. 'Wood' corresponds to wood which exists, in fact, as wood. However, to say this real wood comes from 'the Hobbiton movie set', which has entered the story here as a small-print advertising-standards risk-management gloss on Middle-earth, is to nudge reliable but boring ontology in the direction of the game. A minimal amount of research on the New Zealand Post website reveals that the piece of 'real wood' is in fact 'particles' from the 'party tree' which featured on the Hobbiton movie set and 'appeared in both *The Lord of the Rings* and *The Hobbit* motion picture trilogies'. These minute material fragments are embedded in images of the 'iconic door to Bag End', the home of Bilbo Baggins. These images with their particles of real pieces from Middle-earth feature on commemorative coins and stamps issued by New Zealand Post, produced in a partnership with Sir Peter Jackson's New Line Cinema and Metro-Goldwyn Mayer (MGM). Their purpose is to promote the final movie in the Middle-earth saga, *The Hobbit: The Battle of the Five Armies*, which opened in December 2014.

The wood is real wood, even if its particles are minute. The Hobbiton movie set also exists: while initially packed down after filming, the set was soon rebuilt solely as a tourist destination, complete with the Green Dragon Inn open for business. What gets it across the advertising-standards anxiety line is an artful conflation of 'location' and 'set'; a location being a place that exists in the 'real world', and a set being an entirely fabricated artefact. The Hobbiton movie set remains a location: a few hectares of farmland near Matamata ('Discover the real Middle-earth at the Hobbiton™ Movie Set near Matamata.' www.hobbitontours.com).

So is this where Middle-earth is located—the Middle-earth of which we are promised a 'real piece'? Not quite, because the location, while a real place, has been production-designed, landscaped and equipped with props (such as the wooden 'party tree'), and has therefore shifted across to that ambiguous zone between location and set, which can in the end only *really* be situated, embodied, in the film experience of it; in the film where, and only where, Middle-earth exists—*really exists*, according to the truth-values of the cinema. A tantalising stretch remains between location at Matamata and Middle-earth on the screen: the situation of the located set, of the place that is simultaneously here and there, in this truth and in that. I guess you could say that religious relics sometimes have this kind of paradoxical existence, at once manifestly and fictionally real—occupying not a liminal but a magical space in which disciplining edges don't count; the space of the movies, for example.

If I purchase the 'presentation pack' of coin and stamp, I go into the draw to win a trip for two to the Hobbiton Movie Set and a picnic under the 'party tree'. The products are of course 'available globally' via nzpost.co.nz/thehobbit, or—and this is the bit I like—from PostShop, REAL Aotearoa, 0800NZstamps.

Distance is now looking every which way, and I know which realist granddaughter will be joining me under the party tree when I win the draw. Bella will be satisfied with the answer that the 'real piece of Middle-earth' comes from a movie about a place that never existed, except that she's there having a picnic, what's your problem? And I'll be satisfied with that answer as well, but, because I'm older, will also know that the meaning and value of the 'real piece' of wood have been generated by the global marketing narratives of a major film production consortium, and a national communications delivery system whose job it is to deliver these meanings and values to its customers who, like the happy picnickers, prefer to believe that there's nothing particularly unusual about this construction of place.

Most of us don't have much trouble feeling at home here. It's what most of us do, most of the time. Happy (maybe unhappy) picnickers in a paradoxical location that may even constitute a new kind of indigeneity, perhaps situated in something like a set of conditions James Clifford has provisionally defined as 'traditional futures'. This, I hasten to add, is not exclusively a modern situation, though its conditions may have been normalised by the proliferation of virtual realities. Film is, after all, 125 years old. But then, *Mahābhārata* has its origins somewhere between the eighth and nineth centuries BCE, and movie adaptations have continued to gush spectacularly from this source since 1920; had Bella been born in India rather than New Zealand, she'd very probably be situated in the latest Bollywood retelling of a story out of *Mahābhārata*.

There's a Twitter version of *Mahābhārata* that will go on eking out its 140 characters through many generations after Bella's, if Twitter survives. Right now *Mahābhārata* is trending on Twitter, in multiple languages and places, and continues to reel the future into a present that persists in playing with the past. Bella will soon outgrow Elsa of *Frozen*, but will continue, let's hope, to essay herself on locations, plural.

Notes on Sources:

Clifford Geertz, 'Thick Description: Towards an Interpretive Theory of Culture', in *The Interpretation of Cultures* (New York: Basic Books, 2000), 6.
Georges Poulet, 'Phenomenology of Reading', in *New Literary History* 1.1 (October 1969) 53–68.
James Clifford, 'Traditional Futures', in *Questions of Tradition*, ed. Mark Phillips and Gordon Schochet (Toronto: University of Toronto Press, 2004), 152–168.

Issues of place dominate **Ian Wedde**'s work, such as in his contribution to the 1985 symposium, *Te Whenua te Iwi/The Land and the People*, many essays in his collections (*How to be Nowhere: Essays and Texts 1971–1994* and *Making Ends Meet: Essays and Talks 1992–2004*), his novels *Symmes Hole* (1986) and *The Viewing Platform* (2006); the 2008 centennial exhibition *He Korowai o te Wai: The Mantle of Water* for the Rotorua Museum of Art and History; and his book-length essay *The Grass Catcher* (2014). A work in progress (*The Little Ache: A German Notebook*) involves the displacement of his German great-grandparents and how they haunt the present. His novel *Trifecta* (2015) explores how the middle-aged children of an immigrant European modernist architect still inhabit situations vectored by their father's iconic family home. Ian lives in Auckland.

Writing the Impersonal Essay, or: Google Knows Where You've Been

Giovanni Tiso

Consider the story overleaf, which appeared on the web in August of 2014.

I say 'story' because it's the word used on the cover, which also identifies me as the author, but if you clicked through you would discover that it's actually a photo album. Twenty-four pictures taken, as the title indicates, on a trip to Camogli and Genoa in early June of that year.

There are no captions, except for a note indicating that the scene has shifted to the marine reserve of Portofino, on the way to the historic abbey of San Fruttuoso—the album's final destination.

None of this is remarkable, except for the following details: I didn't compile the album of which I was claimed to be the author; I didn't choose the title nor pick the image on the cover; I didn't even ask for the album to be created, nor

JUNE 2, 2014 · 2 DAYS
Trip to Camogli and Genoa

A STORY BY Giovanni Tiso (>)

Change cover photo

Add a caption

was I aware that it would be until it appeared one day on the social network Google+. All I did was take the pictures and upload them to my laptop, in a folder that happens to be connected to my Google Drive, a cloud storage service offered by the company.

My first reaction upon seeing this was of slight bewilderment. I barely use my Google+ account and was not aware of Stories, its facility for creating albums from the holiday pictures taken by its users. At first, however, I was mostly baffled that Google was able to tell so precisely where I had been. I took the pictures with a regular digital camera, not with a location-enabled smartphone. The camera did have a GPS function, but I deactivated it as soon as I left the shop. Yet the album was perfectly accurate: I had been to Camogli and Genoa, and crossed into the marine reserve of Portofino just as indicated.

I did some research. The new feature had been introduced earlier that

year without actively alerting Google+ users, although the official Google blog published a post entitled 'Memories Made Easier', in which the company explained how Stories would take the work out of sifting through holiday photos and videos, automatically weaving them 'into a beautiful travelogue'. As for the part where they could tell where I had been, the company is a little more reserved, but it is reasonable to assume that its landmark detection feature played a part, as well as the company's constantly expanding global database of user-supplied pictures with GPS data through its ownership of the image-sharing service Picasa. Genoa, San Fruttuoso and Camogli are all popular tourist destinations and would be easily recognised by the landmark detection algorithms or matched through the archives. But what about the marine reserve? In this case the location detection could well have been triggered by the following picture:

San Fruttuoso can only be reached by boat or by hiking across a hill. This is a clearing you reach during the walk, on the way down to the bay, making it a natural landmark of sorts and a very obvious picture to take.

In other words: how Google knows where I was in the first week of June 2014 is because there are a lot of people like me who upload or back up our pictures onto the company's servers. Letting the company play with the content they store for us is a sometimes tacit, sometimes explicit, part of the transaction. Furthermore—time-saving convenience being the wonderful thing that it is—I am confident that many, if not most, users will be happy with the features that are added from time to time, and that they never knew they needed. Like the wonderfully named 'Auto Awesome', to which Stories is the latest addition.

One of the most striking functions of Auto Awesome consists in taking several portraits in your collection and combining them to produce an improved composite. Say there is a picture of you smiling with your eyes closed, quickly followed by another in the same pose but in which your eyes are open: Auto Awesome will take the most desirable features of the two images to reproduce a moment that never existed in time. But who cares? It is a beautiful picture, and you're in it.

'Memories made easier' is an attractive-sounding proposition. I should stress that we're dealing strictly about social memory here. This is what stories are about: sharing our experiences and interests, so that others may know us better. But this is also how we construct our identity, socially, and has been since long before these new technologies.

Therein lies my second reaction: namely, the feeling of having been intruded upon, of having had my privacy violated.

What Google doesn't and—thankfully—couldn't know, is that I took that trip to Camogli and Genoa a week after burying my mother. It was during a brief, unscheduled lull before the flight back to New Zealand that I had booked in haste when the phone call came. I left Milan by train to get away from the painful familiarity of the apartment and the streets where I grew up. I chose San Fruttuoso because Mum had been a long-time supporter of the Italian Fund for the Environment, which had financed and overseen its restoration, but was never able to visit it herself, due to how difficult it is to get there.

While taking those pictures, I was thinking of both of my parents, who taught me to love art and to find peace and comfort in such places, which I was seeing, I think, through their eyes and with their sensibilities.

Reduced to a set of 24 pictures without commentary, that trip as it was presented to me by Google meant something else, something less. Stripped of its emotional content, it became a trite account of a holiday like any other, which could have been taken by anyone—which is in fact precisely how Google could tell where I had been.

If these were memories, they weren't mine. Delivered two months later, out of the blue, and demanding that I acknowledge them as part of my life, they felt unreal.

Nevertheless, I published the album on my idle, hollow Google+ profile, to hang on to it a bit longer and figure out how they did it. Later it occurred to me that I could go on allowing Google to document every future trip of mine in this way, and find myself, years from now, with a perfect record of the life of a perfect stranger.

What Stories does by making memories easier is to take up some of the work of autobiography. We could call it the impersonal essay: a system of templates and algorithms for keeping a first-person, intimate record of our lives. The palimpsest offered by Stories consists of pictures, but there is no reason why in the future its repertoire couldn't be expanded to include text as well.

Consider machine translations. Traditional attempts to get computers to translate texts were based on getting them to develop an understanding of natural language and grammar, if not semantics. These attempts proved to be largely fruitless. The much more successful machine translation tools available today—the most widely used of which belongs, again, to Google—rely instead on leveraging a vast and growing corpus of texts translated by humans in order to analyse sentences and produce the most statistically likely equivalent in the target language. The idea is that if most translators have translated a certain type of sentence in a certain way, that wording will likely produce correct translations in the majority of contexts. Thus one finds that tools like Google Translate are increasingly effective at providing the very thing that used to elude computers: namely, the general sense, or gist, of a text, if not always the subtlety of each individual sentence.

It is possible that Stories already operates by making statistical inferences about user preference when selecting the most appealing photographs to publish: how else would you teach a machine to make an aesthetic judgement? It is also not a great stretch to presume that soon the feature may not just choose the title, as it already does, but also offer captions for the photographs, based on the location and any landmarks it might recognise.

The next step would be to provide the accompanying text, that is to say the essay proper. It is a much bigger leap, but remember that both Facebook and Google have been analysing personal utterances for years, having built their extraordinary fortunes on matching advertising to the words most frequently typed by their users. Statistical algorithms could extract from this already existing and almost unimaginably large database the most common phrases found in social media status updates associated with visiting certain places and taking certain pictures, then stitch them together into the beginnings of an essay, if not the whole thing. After all, computers already produce entire media articles about simple, highly repetitive events such as the daily round-ups of the global stock markets. We might find that our holidays—outside of extraordinary circumstances such as the ones I found myself in when I visited Liguria—aren't much less predictable.

You may think it far-fetched, and I do too, although largely because I suspect it would be considered too invasive by users. Yet the fully fledged impersonal essay is certainly within the technical realm of possibility.

The second point I want to make is the inverse of the first: forget about computers writing your autobiography, and focus instead on the extent to which autobiographical writing as a genre is being reshaped by social media.

The internet is, it seems to me, above all, a rhetorical engine. It has created platforms and templates for personal writing that didn't exist before, and in so doing has drawn into the public domain genres that used to be largely private, such as the personal diary or epistle.

At the time of writing, Facebook has close to one and a half billion users, and will almost certainly have exceeded this number by the time of printing. Many, if not most, of them—or I should say *us*, given as I am on Facebook—engage in a running, open-ended, extemporaneous sort of personal essay. I don't mean any of this pejoratively: I view the fact that more people than ever have the means and opportunity to write about themselves and comment on culture, politics and society as a very positive thing. Yet we should also reflect upon the extent to which the particular tools that are available to us, and which are shaped in turn in large part by the means of extracting profit from them, are writing their subjects.

If I publish with little or no changes the story of my trip to Camogli and Genoa, I am allowing Google to describe my experience. But equally, if I keep a record of my life and opinions through Facebook or Twitter, I will do so within the deep grooves of those mediums, with a frequency and in a language likely to be dictated by their need to consume more and more content from more and more people. Life in 140-character chunks, or in the form of status updates, is already a kind of impersonal essay.

Place plays a central role in this, as the phrase 'I was here'—in words, pictures or both—is the basic utterance of this genre. This is why, as opposed to how, Google wrote the story of my trip: it knew I was there, and assumed that I would want to tell people about it, because that's what people do. It was a reasonable assumption, although it failed to account for my reasons for being in that place at that time. The story—the *real* story—was hidden, or perhaps suspended, in the space between the pictures.

I can see no larger lesson in all this, save for the reminder that personal essay-writing is always contingent on an epoch's technologies of writing as well as to social realities and pressures; and that we should guard against the most subtle, insidious constraints on what we can think and say about ourselves. The existence of dominant rhetorical forms, which at the present time loom very large, is also an implicit invitation to find ways to go against the grain, to resist being reduced to a statistical norm: it is from that resistance that we can find insight and learn to say that which is not obvious, and that a machine couldn't guess.

Notes on Sources:

'Google+ Stories and Movies: memories made easier.' *Google Official Blog,* 20 May 2014, Accessed 23 August 2015. <http://googleblog.blogspot.co.nz/2014/05/google-stories-and-movies-memories-made.html>

Giovanni Tiso is an Italian writer and translator based in Wellington. He completed a PhD in English Literature at Victoria University in 2006 on the relationship between memory and technology. Two years later he began blogging at *Bat, Bean, Beam* (http://bat-beanbeam.blogspot.co.nz) as a way of continuing his research and bringing it to a wider public. Over time, a strand of the essays on the blog became steadily more personal, initially in connection with the issue of the transmission of family memory and his yearly trips back home to Italy. Giovanni's essays have been published by *The New Inquiry*, *The New Humanist* and *Sport*, as well as in the first two editions of the nonfiction anthology *Tell You What*. Since 2012 he has been a featured writer of the Australian literary magazine *Overland*.

There Is No Up, There Is No Down

Tim Corballis

Why this image? It resembles the desktop background of the computer used for presentations during the *Placing the Personal Essay* colloquium. That image came up repeatedly on the room's large screen during the day, in between the various slideshows. At the beginning of my own talk, I asked for it to be left up for a moment, but I didn't say very much about it except, as I recall, *there's* a place. A galaxy is a place. In a relatively spontaneous way, I liked that this image, with its vast, distanced scale was the thing that punctuated all of the small, close stories we had been hearing. It was vast and distanced, but in no way abstract. A galaxy is as real and as concrete as a local shop or a hotel or a stream.

I've found myself thinking lately about the idea of leaving the earth's surface. It's somewhere between a fantasy and a reality. We can leave the earth,

but we never get very far from it. Most of us use planes to get from one part of the surface to another. We do get perspectives on the surface from space, from a great height, but the actual departure—that's the fantasy.

I fantasised about it when I was a child. I suppose I was in some ways a typical boy, into *Star Wars* and *Star Trek* and all kinds of space stuff. Maybe there was some compensation in them for some dissatisfaction with my life. Not in any profound way, of course. My upbringing was middle-class, comfortable and suburban, my family supportive and loving. There was nothing horrific, no need to become an 'internal emigrant'. I suspect it was fairly normal childhood escapism. The addition of drama to an undramatic life—isn't that one of the functions of stories?

I was mostly interested in the cerebral side of those TV programmes and films. I wasn't attracted to the fantasy of interstellar war, of a hypertrophied male body, superhero stuff and violence. I was more interested in Mr Spock, in the megabrain and the nerdy idea that the mind might have power of its own. This was a kind of mental magic, a kind of philosophical idealism, the meshing of thought and world. Space is a good place for it, since it's all about an empty space, weightlessness and frictionlessness. I think it's where matter acts a bit like thought. Objects collide and rebound like they're supposed to in the equations; fields extend smoothly through emptiness. I'm not even sure all of that is true. It's very appealing, this outer space. It is both the space inside which we are all suspended on our small planet, but also the space inside our minds—as if, thinking large, we think the universe. It's a certain kind of thought, and not the only kind. In a lot of ways, of course, apart from the shreds of evidence that fall to us here, thought is the only way we know about space, about the universe. So it's also inhuman. It's the space of a certain kind of thought, but it's the space in which we are irrelevant, the space we can't occupy.

Tell us about your background in mathematics?

It's a bit grand to call it a background. I studied mathematics and physics when I first went to university. Mathematics and theoretical physics are both things that take place in a kind of empty space of thought. When I began studying, they still had a sort of romantic appeal, a hangover from that illusion about the mind, about a magic of the mind. The scripts and symbols helped—symbolic languages of logic and calculus; the various forms of integral shown by different, esoteric swirls. They were like magical writing. The idea of thought and space being related is also something to do with the idea that language has a power over the world. That's among other things a political ideal, a communist one perhaps, one that we no longer have much faith in. But it's also the fantasy of Bill Gates, who believes in a 'frictionless capitalism', or of Apple's creation of a whole symbolic empty space in which the lightest gesture, the touch of a sensitive surface can alter worlds on the screen. So maybe the communist ideal is alive after all, even in Apple, even in Bill Gates.

When I gave up on mathematics it was because I slowly realised that there was no magic in it that could reach out from the empty thought-space and into the world, not without getting into all kinds of 'worldly' areas that I wasn't interested in: engineering, policy and so forth.

Floating in darkness? No, so of course the view from space, the view of space, all this should tell us something about ourselves to be interesting. There's at the very least a kind of negative theological view inherent in it: the very lack of magic, the fact that empty space is just empty, and that we are not anywhere near the centre of it, that we are a tiny portion of it.

Maps.

Maps involve a fantasy of leaving the earth's surface, of looking at it from above. I thought about maps first as part of the writing I did for Fiona Amundsen's photographic exhibition *Operation Magic*, which became part of her project *The Imperial Body*. Her work was and is focusing on the Second World War in the Pacific, and I began to think about how that war, particularly from the United States' point of view, gave the Pacific Ocean a new cartography. It became about territory to be captured from or ceded to the Japanese. I was writing about how oceans become territory—how they become just the same as land in some way. This had something to do with the threat of Japanese invasion, with Pearl Harbour (*Operation Magic* was a series of Pearl Harbour photographs), which expanded America's strategic claim on the earth's surface further west from its west coast. Some time around then, too, planes began to justify different kinds of maps from those used by ships—azimuthal rather than Mercator projections, partly because they were better suited to polar regions. Ice was no impediment to planes, the way it was to ships, and a great deal of the 'global war' was a northern hemisphere war, mappable from a point directly above the North Pole. Azimuthal projections represented the earth as a circle rather than a rectangle, so they gave a much clearer sense of height, height above a particular point on a sphere. The whole century progressively refined our sense of the planet as a sphere. From the flights of the great aviators to commercial air travel, all of this closed the globe, wrapped it up. But in general there were more and more aerial views, or views pretending to be aerial. There was *Earthrise*, of course, an extreme example. Landsat imagery became available at some point in the 70s I think, and then unavoidable in the form of Google Maps images. In the last few years—I'm not sure when—the ocean floor has been viewable on Google Maps, though not in huge detail yet. It looks wonderful. It is possible to see the ocean's mountains, ridges and caverns. It is more territory, more ocean become earth. It looks like the surface of another planet.

Are our heightened imaginings of the world colonial?

Yes. I think the various kinds of map projections have overlaid another kind of spatial imagination. Think of Tuki's map, drawn by Tuki Te Terenui Whare Pirau in 1793. That's a hybrid map, using the conventions of Western mapmaking but not its geometrical projections—it's like many similar maps, drawn by people to give others instructions, say. Its most obvious feature is that scale diminishes rapidly in proportion to the distance from Tuki's rohe, so that coastlines nearby are drawn large and in a lot of detail, while ones further off are sketched in, small and simple. It's in some ways a map of an understanding of the world, a perspectival map. It shares this feature with azimuthal projections, except you could argue that it is more human in scale, and doesn't involve height above the earth's surface so much as a picture built up from the surface or from head-height: from movement and trade conducted on it, knowledge of it.

But the point about mathematical projections—artificial constructions,

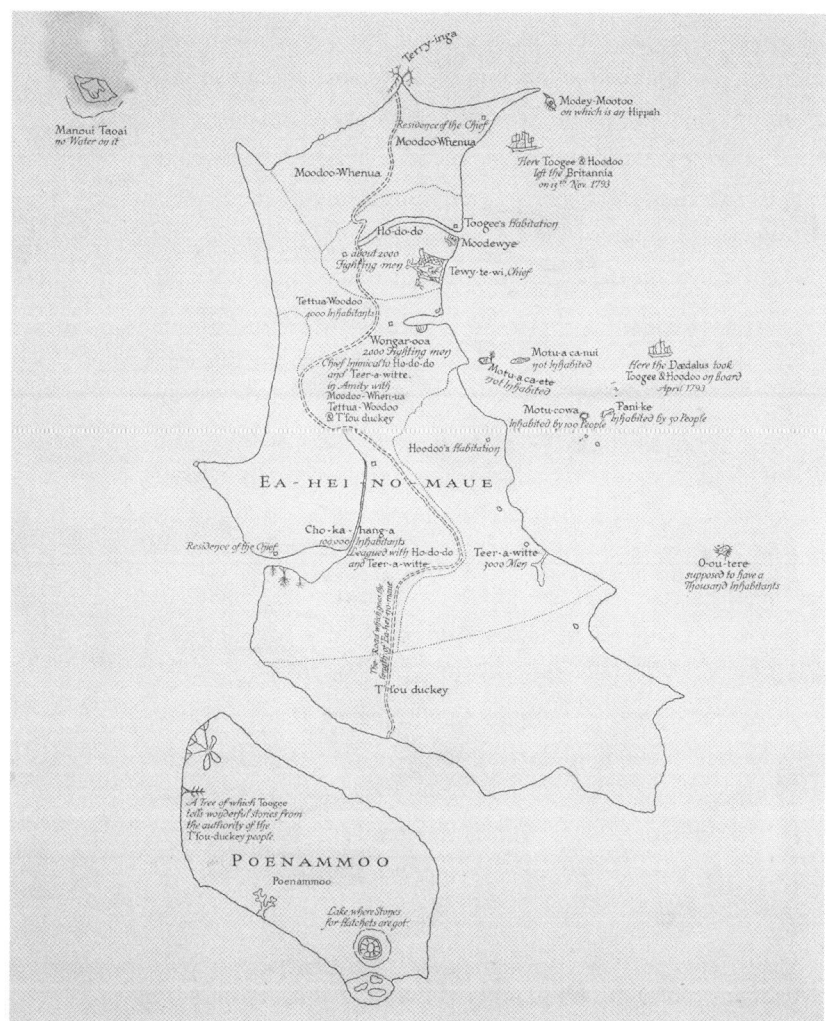

Milligan, Robert Roy Douglas, 1893–1962. New Zealand Department of Internal Affairs Centennial Publications Branch: Tuki's map [copy of ms map]. [ca.1940]. Originally by Tuki Te Terenui Whare Pirau, b. 1769?. New Zealand Department of Internal Affairs Centennial Publications Branch: Maps from Historical Atlas. Ref: MapColl-CHA-2/1/9-Acc.36440. Alexander Turnbull Library, Wellington, New Zealand. http://natlib.govt.nz/records/22866321

really, of a heightened view—is that they can come in and obliterate the kind of spatial imagination embodied in Tuki's map. They are used to say, I guess, that Tuki's map, though interesting, is wrong. They are used to say that Tuki's place is not as large as he thinks—in fact, from the perspective of the globe, see how tiny it is . . . It's actually far smaller than Te Waipounamu, which Tuki draws as a small rectangle. Maps, then, can neutralise places and discipline people, give them a sense of powerlessness in the face of the larger mapped territory and ultimately the globe. This is quite apart from any practical uses that maps have in commoditising land.

Of course every technology, every image has a different meaning depending on its use and its context. We can't just be against maps and height-perspectives, any more than we can be for them. Doreen Massey, for example, makes use at least once of the 'outer space' perspective. She says, if you were on a satellite looking down at earth, you'd see all this movement, all these different kinds of movement reflecting differences in class, gender and so on.[1] She makes the point, in the passage I'm thinking about, by leaving the earth's surface in her imagination. This is a kind of whole-earth perspective, a mapping perspective that is able to see relations and mobilities that might not be so visible from the ground, metaphorically speaking. For all the human geographer's loyalty to the earth, she leaves it in order to see it.

If a place is a place only in relation to other places, you have to leave that place so it can become a place.

Leaving the earth's surface makes the world and the places in it into something different. This can work in a lot of ways. *Earthrise* and other images of the earth from space have been used, as for example on the covers of the *Whole Earth Catalogues* from the late 1960s, to suggest something that I think is both valuable and wrong: that we are all together on this planet, that we are all connected to one another. Massey's experience on the satellite was a sophisticated version of this: look at the connections, and also at the differences and the different kinds of connections. But the banal hippy version is right in its own way too. Every time we start a car and release carbon dioxide into the atmosphere, we affect, if you like, every single other person on the planet. Not all in the same way, of course—poor people affect and are affected in different ways from rich people, coastal people differently from those in the mountains, people in the tropics differently from those in temperate zones. It is only possible to think about global warming, to understand the possibility of it and to develop a science of it, if we have an understanding and, I daresay, an image of the earth as a whole.

Every time we breathe or light a fire or start a car, there is the earth. We are on it, the invisibly large thing, and it hangs visibly in front of us as if by striking the match or turning the ignition we can touch it with our hands. This is both a fact and a remarkable everyday short circuit of the imagination. Without the rockets that sent machines and people into space, rockets that themselves visibly spewed their exhaust into the air, could we even conceive of what is happening?

What kind of place do you think the world can be?

Here is one version of a place: the classical agora, say, the meeting place for democracy. Every time we undertake a hīkoi we are re-enacting the potential implicit in that place. It is a place that means 'everyone together'; it is a place that allows all people, irrespective of their places in the hierarchy, to present themselves as bodies and as decision-makers. In that place is the hope for a disentanglement and an assertion of will by the people. In that place, real entanglements of power and economics are cut through, in favour of the political possibilities of encounter. I wrote about this kind of place in my doctoral thesis—a place defined by being together, coming together, and a place defined by democratic claim. It's as good a model for politics as I know, and it works by explicit contrasts: contrasting the people, the demonstrators, with the corruption of government, emphasising that the meaning of the crowd is 'everyone' even if only a few thousand people are actually present, and that existing power is always held in the interests of the few. I'm not sure if it's an effective politics, working mostly at the level of symbols and seldom actually displacing hierarchies and interests. But it happens in a place that is defined by the lack of place, the departure of people from their proper place (the response of the police is always, 'Go home to where you belong.')[2]

The view of the globe—this makes the world into a singular place, as if all of humanity had come together. It is a kind of demonstration—false, if it forgets the divisions and entanglements and hierarchies and abuses that take place on its surface (as if 'humanity', rather than a specific set of economic/ecological practices, were the cause of global warming), but true if it presents a CLAIM on behalf of all its people, on behalf of *everyone* against all of those hierarchies. This is what the globe can mean: a place against places, a vision of the world's people, a vision that we can hold up in opposition to power.

A shift in perspective then; but it moves us towards fragility, too—nakedness. The body faced with another body, aware that things such as privilege are, in the long view, easily stripped away.

The view from space reveals that we are in a vacuum; it reveals the atmosphere as only the thinnest layer of breathable air, easily stripped from the planet's surface by the solar wind were it not for the good fortune of a strong magnetic field. Vacuum means precisely that there is nothing in between two objects—not air, not ether, not space itself. Objects spin space out of themselves—they do not exist *in* it (versions of this lesson are found in both Einstein and Lefebvre).

Leaving the earth means that what we think of as backgrounds are shifted forwards. It shows us that the very idea of background is false. There are things and people, held in highly complex relations to one another; but we do well not to let all of those relations, the power and accommodation and compromise, slip into the background again as *what is*. Bringing them forward means we acknowledge that we touch much more than we see. When we look for the hidden essence of a place, I suspect what we find first is landscape painting, background music and land title, a product of people's power over one another. Instead, turn off the music, forget the place in favour of what we coexist with: families and strangers, taniwha and ancestors, stones and water, flora and fauna.

These are the things our essays could be responsive to?

I think so. Moreover, we are faced always, and in increasingly important ways, with distant and invisible things. There is the challenge: we can no longer rely on our senses. So also: carbon and nitrogen, the magnetosphere and UV light, habit and language and culture (things coded in our bodies).

It is better, in any case, to be responsive than to be evocative. Evocation brings a place into being as palpable, a matter of the senses but so much of importance is not perceptible. The evoked place, the scene, is, from any larger perspective, an accident, a temporary thing, and the evocation makes it seem like a permanent background. This coincidence of light and surfaces will be gone before long. There's nothing wrong with enjoying it while it lasts (maybe thousands of years) but in any case, the light, the air, the fish, none of it comes from here. When we dig to find the essence of a place, there is no point at which our digging reaches a firm foundation. We will always dig further.

Perhaps we could say this: the point of our essays is not to carry us in the imagination to another place. They might, instead, enable us to look up at the place we are in, to look through it and out of it. They might enable us to locate ourselves in a place outside of place, in some hidden coexistence . . .

Notes on Sources:

1   Doreen Massey, *Space, Place and Gender* (Minneapolis: Minnesota University Press, 1994), 148–9.

2   This follows the politics of Jacques Rancière. See especially *Disagreement: Politics and Philosophy* (Minneapolis: University of Minnesota Press, 1999).

Tim Corballis is a writer based in Wellington. He is the author of four novels, most recently *R.H.I.* (Wellington: Victoria University Press, 2015), as well as a large number of shorter works including short fiction, reviews, essays and art writing. His essay 'Winter' won the 2013 *Landfall* essay competition. He has been collaborating with photographer Fiona Amundsen since 2004, on works such as 'Si C'est' ('If It Is') (2007, shown at The Physics Room, Christchurch and Te Tuhi, Auckland) and the video work 'Machine Wind' (2015, shown at Te Tuhi, Auckland). He has completed a doctorate through the University of Auckland, focusing on the possibilities of aesthetic theory in antipodean contexts. In 2015 he was the Victoria University of Wellington/Creative New Zealand Writer in Residence.

Speculative Geographies

Response Essay: PlaceTime

Martin Edmond

In 1981, at the dental hospital in Sydney, I had a near-death experience. Or maybe it was an out-of-body excursion. It happened after a needle full of anaesthetic was driven into my gum. While the details of the procedure—an apicoectomy—are unimportant, there are aspects to the event that still seem apposite. Specifically, the way I came back from a period of unconsciousness of unknown duration. It seemed that I could return only by locating, in a geographical sense, the place of genesis of the body, mind and soul which I possess or which possess me. I had to know where I come from in order to continue to be.

The experience was planetary. Ascending rapidly, looking down, I saw below me the town of Ohakune. From a point of origin at the house in Burns Street where I grew up, a map of the familiar streets—the Tohunga Road, Old Station Road, Clyde Street, Goldfinch Street, the Raetihi Road—unfolded, precise, redolent, miniaturising as I went higher. I was flying west. I saw Ruapehu and its satellite cones like pustules erupting from the earth; the dissected bush-covered hill country of the Whanganui; Taranaki another snow-girt boil; the ochre cliffs and black sand beaches of the wild west coast; the endless unquiet broken waters of the Tasman Sea.

The sandstones of the Bondi shore loomed up, the orange-roofed houses with their aqua swimming pools, the massed terraces of Paddington and the warehouses of Surry Hills, passing by below, getting larger—and then I was in, in the window, into the room in which my body lay, there, upon the dentist's chair. A gasp of breath—*Tihei, mauri ora!*—and I was back. The endodontist and the half-dozen students he was instructing were gazing down at me, the circle their heads made slowly revolving. He was slapping my face. *Come on, man, come on!* For a moment I did not know where or who or what I was.

But those questions had already been answered in the journey, surely only seconds long, I had just made. In extremis, the only way to maintain continuity of self was through a reprise of origins followed by a return to where 'I' was situated. Nowadays we tend to think of ourselves as psychologically, then socially, configured. There are aspects we don't attend to much anymore: mythic, chthonic. Genii locus. An unfashionable notion but not without precedent: we are made, in a material sense, from our native place. Its water and air, its soil and food. I realised in that brief out-of-body experience that we are not, as we like to think, merely a who or a what: we are also a where.

For many of us, however, place is buried in time; even if that time be the present. Some kind of excavation is required. Or, a decoding. As to future places, they are prospective and so equivocal: something yet to be realised that may or may not come into being. *Who's your name?* the kids used to ask me when I moved to a new town. *Where you from?* This might be followed by: *Where you stay?* Which interrogations encompass time, space and identity. You have a name. You come from somewhere; you live there still or you live in another place. Between those two designations, if they are not the same—and for most of us now they are not—there is a personal history which is probably without much significance.

Communities are different; those questions are really asking for the story of your people, where they are from, how they fit in with other peoples. Family, the street your house is in, the school you go or went to, the town where you live, the one you lived in before, what work you do, the larger groups with which, howsoever tenuously, you are affiliated: these are of consuming interest to anyone you come across, no doubt so that they can match them, or not, with their own.

This is where memory comes in: to my mind as much a provocation to storytelling as a means of recall. But memory must be searched: how is this to be done? An archive is implied, though it is an organic archive, subject to the vagaries of all soft machines, made as they are of chemicals and blood and tissue. And one, moreover, without a cataloguing system; unless the storytelling we do with respect to memory is itself an impulse towards ordering; which I suppose it is. Here the fiction/nonfiction divide breaks irretrievably down; and a good thing too.

Then there are the archives themselves; their physicality. Stone, bone, baked clay, papyrus, vellum, paper, magnetic disks, code, all containing information we believe can in some sense be verified. We also know that it can be transcribed and made into something else. Paradoxically, however, whatever their usefulness, items in an archive always bear witness to other items which have been lost. Archives are full of absences and thus as questionable as memories. Those lost and found things: are they holy writ or just another provocation for storytelling?

Writing may be sacred in its origins, but it is always also a record of something that needed to be preserved against the inevitable decay—commemoration of a debt, rehearsal of a prayer, reification of a name. Yet preservation itself turns out to be a random process, whereby many copies of some texts are retained alongside those which are unique: we have Tacitus's two major works in an incomplete single copy of each; manuscripts of Homer begin as fragments of verses inscribed on vases and go on from there into a pleroma of versions which seem to exist simultaneously in writing and in memory; so that voices wake in the mind and start telling those ancient tales along with us as we read.

The argument about ownership of the shared ground between archive and memory may be resolved: if you think of each as a vector from past to future then they are clearly on convergent trajectories. I suggest that archives are as questionable as memory and may be interrogated in the same rigorous fashion as we interrogate recall; but that they also, and likewise, return to us images as various and strange as those that appear in dreams. To investigate something properly we need all three: archives, dreams, memories. And once we have arrived at an idea of what we think the truth of the matter might be, then it may be written out as story. And so the liberation of a collection like this becomes possible.

Place is always specific: a there, not a somewhere, an elsewhere, a nowhere. Or is it? One thing quickly became apparent as I read through these essays: the places we think and write about are time-specific as well—a when as well as a where. Te Kūiti in the late 1990s is not the same Te Kūiti where Te Kooti and his band lived more than a hundred years before. Nor is post-earthquake Christchurch the same as its pre-catastrophe precursor. Not the same; but not really distinct either. Just as pre-earthquake Napier is discernible beneath what has been made of the land that rose up in 1931, so the past of any place persists into the present and may, especially if noted, form a part of the future. When we write place, then, we are also writing time. They are dancing partners performing a complex pas de deux in our minds, where they make an intimate, intricate entanglement that might be called placetime.

In writing, any kind of writing, it is never really now. Not even at this moment, when I look out the window and see the preternatural green of storm-washed eucalypt leaves against the purple-grey sky: because, by the time anyone else reads that sentence, it will be speaking of the past. And the Ohakune I saw, when was that? The sadly derelict town it was in 1981? Or the rather more thriving one I knew when we left in 1962? Or some composite which includes both versions, indeed all versions, from when the bush was felled up until, and beyond, the booming ski-town and summer resort it is now becoming?

There is an acute melancholy to be found in the contemplation of the ways in which places change over time; and an equal, and opposite, melancholy to be experienced in those places that do not change, or do not appear to do so. Both speak of exile. That town of my youth is irrecoverable now, or recoverable only in memory; while the mountain that stands over it, seemingly eternal, only emphasises how much I myself have changed, how far away that lost boyhood is. The point remains: as soon as we begin to write place, we also begin writing time, even if that time is just the history of a self.

Here is a clue as to why the personal essay, expertly showcased in this collection, has become one of the more flexible forms available to those who write: because it allows the use of the cognisant self as the instrument by which and through which we make our inquiries. This doesn't mean the self is the focus of inquiry; far from it. Those works that take as their subject matter a writer's own sensibility now seem irretrievably old-fashioned, belonging to an earlier, more privileged, era. The self as instrument remains viable, however, because its volatility, its provisional nature, its multifariousness, may be both admitted and utilised. Even when the subject of the inquiry is memory or dream—that is, the mind inquiring of itself—the divisive and contradictory nature of consciousness is immediately foregrounded.

Likewise a mind at work in an archive is always more interesting than either archive or mind, considered separately. Archives, as mentioned, are paradoxical. They witness what is lost as much as what is preserved; and that which does survive is never the whole story. They are also, despite the best of intentions, impermanent. Recently I read through a series of telegraphed despatches sent to British newspapers from Petrograd between the death of Rasputin in late 1916 and the ratification of the Treaty of Brest-Litovsk in March, 1918. They told, in incomparable, riveting detail, the story of the Russian revolution.

But here was a disturbing thing: the paper on which these despatches were typed had gone thin and brown with the years and each one threatened to crumble to dust as it was picked up: a visible sign of the disintegration all material, howsoever made, is subject to. Mortality, in a word. Each day as I left the library there was on the desk I worked at and on the floor beneath it a residue, a papery accretion which, as I scanned the room, turned out not to be mine alone but an addition to that left behind by other researchers. These papers, which had been typed in Petrograd a hundred years before, were now becoming dust on the floor of a library in New York. They told the story of the revolution; but were themselves part of another story, the one I was attempting to tell: the biography of the man who wrote them.

In biography, it seems to me, time and place are intrinsic; but it is also the case that we have contrary notions of these two matrices: we tend to think of place as physical and therefore, while subject to change, in some sense durable. 'Rolled round on earth's diurnal course/with rocks, and stones, and trees,' as Wordsworth put it. Time, by contrast, is insubstantial, a process; it is evanescent, a quantity in which events occur, not a thing in itself. Is it not strange that when we look to one we see the other? Place, then, is in some sense to be understood as a particular location known through an examination of the ways in which it has changed, or endured, over time.

Another thing. Places are important to us because we feel there is something eternal to them; something that is outside of time. The eels Alice Te Punga Somerville writes about in her essay have, immemorially, lived in the Waitangi stream that runs beneath that part of Wellington south of where Te Papa now stands, and live there still. They survived the disruption of the lagoon by the 1855 earthquake, and the subsequent confining of the waters of the stream within pipes. They keep coming back to the same place as if nothing has changed. Time may have altered the place, but not their habitation of it.

Eels don't actually live outside of time but, like many denizens of what we call the natural world, and indeed like 'nature' itself, they seem to witness time not as a series of discrete events with a beginning and an end, but as a repetitive, indeed cyclical process, which rehearses itself indefinitely and is always the same and always different. We humans are profoundly attracted to this notion of cyclical time, and, equally, these days, profoundly alienated from its actual unfolding. The sense of a natural world that is cyclical, repetitive, self-healing, whole, would seem to have something to do with our attachment to specific, perhaps natal, places: as if there, and only there, can we truly, wholly, locate ourselves, even though we might spend the majority of our lives elsewhere.

This must be because the places we have known become reconfigured within as a part of us, a part, that is, of our psyche. Those places we have known are 'in' us, just as we may feel a part of us is 'in' the places we have known. It is well understood that time is mutable, that we experience it psychologically as much as in the outward manifestations it may have, or seem to have. Place, this collection makes clear, is like that too. We can, and frequently do, revisit in memory places we have loved, places we have been and cannot go again, places that once existed and now no longer do. We even visit places that have never existed, or do not yet exist, or may never exist: alternate realities, dream states, futures.

In fact our minds are, to an almost alarming extent, archives of places we know, have known, might yet know. Common sense suggests that the ability to configure places is likely a very ancient skill, or proclivity, and one that we share with many other creatures. Migratory birds come to mind. Or incredible journeys undertaken by lost pets. Those eels. These places can be prospective or retrospective, but their actual making is always in the present. So we might say that it is our *consciousness* of place that is at issue here, not the places themselves; and then go a step further and suggest that places, in this sense if not in others, might themselves have agency. If we are coeval with place, then the influence places have upon us is equal to, if opposite from, the influence we have upon them. This is where we enter the strange and estranging domain of psychogeography.

A real place might thus have a determining effect upon the denouement of a story: a staple trope of the haunted house tale. Here we seem to cross over, as it were, from past to future. Here what has happened previously makes something, usually untoward, happen now. Or again. The entanglements of the past reach out and make the future different from what it might otherwise have been. Jorge Luis Borges, using a spatial metaphor, called this proliferation of possible futures the garden of forking paths. This does not suggest an enduring, comforting version of a past place as home, whether in memory or in fact; rather it gives a sense that human acts alter places in such a way that an influence may be transmitted to people yet to come, who must either resist or succumb to whatever the past dictates. We are haunted as much by where we have been as by what we have done there.

Invented places are mutable also, suggesting again that psychic forces have real-world effects, even if we do not properly understand what those psychic forces are nor how they operate. Indeed, we seem able to know them only by their effects: the pathology of hoarding is as mysterious as the metamorphoses of stones. Perhaps a biographer maps the changes in the life of a subject as a way of approaching, if not quite reaching, the meaning(s) of his or her own peregrinations, both in terms of geography—the places where s/he has lived—and what might be called the evolution of being. How do we become who we are and what part did our travels play in that? Have we even become who we are—yet? Can we? Devolution is as much a threat 'here' as it might be 'elsewhere': we can never know exactly who we are, or who we were, or who we will be, just as we don't entirely comprehend the places where that 'who' manifests or decays or transforms. In part this must be because all places, whatever their actual status, have a fictional element to them.

Or perhaps by 'fictional' I really mean 'imaginative'? Those identifications— mountain, river, parental name(s)—that Māori use to say who they are and where they come from, make claims that are at once real and mythic too. Pākehā can and sometimes do make the attempt, both poignant and absurd, to recite their own affiliations in te reo; these inevitably lack conviction and seem to need to come along with an apology. Concepts like tūrangawaewae, papakāinga and ahi kā can serve a metaphorical function, I suppose, though in essence they are not metaphorical at all but, if not exactly material, then at least literal. A place to stand, a fire burning, motherland: these have a felt truth, a psychic reality that is particular, not general, and thus not really available for purposes of comparison or co-option.

Or so we like to believe. Pākehā attempts to inhabit these concepts, to live within them, are probably bound to fail; but, given the enviable progress (at least from an Australian perspective) Aotearoa has made towards biculturalism, they are an inevitable result of the exchanges by which biculturalism proceeds. And it is worth noting, I think, again from the point of view of an expatriate, how naturally New Zealanders now use words like whanau or whakapapa. 'Family', 'genealogy', sound differently upon the ear.

Māori may of course find themselves as dislocated, as alienated, as Pākehā; yet here, too, we encounter a paradox. The other side of alienation is belonging, dislocation implies location and resolution may lead to a kind of richness: not one place to stand but many; not a single identity but a multiplicity of possible selves. The individual may be configured, not as an isolate, willing and prospective agent but as a site where networks converge; a nexus in a web of connection—which is to evoke another concept that seems to be in the process of transmuting from the metaphorical to the literal. I mean of course the world wide web.

It would be interesting to know when the word Place started to be used as a singular abstract noun, often with a capital letter, and surely after the analogy with Time. It is a usage that doesn't quite convince, perhaps because Place is made of places in a way that Time is not really made of times. However the coinage, if that's what it is, does seem appropriate in other ways: we now all live in a single place, called Earth, while spending a large part of our time in an areal place, called cyberspace: part dream, part encyclopaedia, part junk, part mind; like DNA perhaps. The global consciousness anticipated by Marshal McLuhan does seem to be evolving, albeit in ways he did not predict and which we cannot always see. We have outsourced so much of our intelligence to a collective, yet we do not quite comprehend what that collective is or might become; nor where our reckless experimentation may lead us.

One of the consequences of this (literal) shift in consciousness is the proliferation of alternative realities, other worlds. Children now grow up assuming a reality to places that began their lives as fictions, inventions, and this is undoubtedly changing their minds. But it is a change back as well as forward: once upon a time used to be where all stories began. That shift might occasion anxiety in some; in others it initiates a prospective voyaging that is characteristic of our species phenomenal (and phenomenological) commitment to the discovery of new places and new ways of seeing. Are we going to shy away this time? I don't think so. We never have before. Whatever lies beyond real or areal horizons retains a seductive promise.

One version of the human past is that it was this, precisely—the thought of what might lie behind the next horizon—that initiated our planet-wide expansion, and there is no reason to think that prospective consciousness has somehow domesticated itself; quite the contrary. Making it up as you go along, implied in all voyages of discovery, has its precise counterpart in the narration of whatever journey you are upon: a possible origin for the essay form. This may be the most difficult way to write successfully but it is surely also the most rewarding; it requires an open mind and an open-ended commitment to whatever might appear before you. The forking paths cannot all be followed, perhaps, but their multitude may be evoked. You might not know where the end is until you reach it; you will not certainly know the path unless you take it. Ontological uncertainty, then, translates into a description of the way that took you to an unforseen end which might (hopefully) turn out to be another beginning.

But the outsourcing of consciousness, of memory, even of dreams, has peculiar, as yet unrealised consequences. How to respond when an algorithm, unbidden, reproduces an account of a personal journey? More and more we are subject to interventions which compose for us a version of who we are, where we come from and where we are going; nevertheless, these narratives are conspicuously anodyne, without affect, without engagement; without inwardness. In them we become the everyman or woman of the rental car advertisement or home kitchen renovation. The interesting thing is what machine-driven functions cannot do: evoke emotion, describe mind, embody soul. We'll have to await further developments in artificial intelligence to see if this remains the case, but I suggest that, however sophisticated robots become, they won't supplant the human, simply because we are animal not machine-based: of a different kind to our inventions.

And exploration of the kind we are? I recall the analogy, so beloved of those who remember the 1960s, between inner and outer space. That vastness we see when we look out at the night sky is echoed by the vastness within. The billions of brain cells we have, to this way of thinking, are like the numberless stars in the observable universe. It is a vague analogy and doesn't really bear scrutiny, but its usefulness in this context is in the way it emphasises the relativity (that word) of both inner and outer space: one is perhaps a mirror of the other, but which is which? External reality, so-called, may perhaps be cancelled out by various means but we cannot easily leave the interior space of the mind, which tends to become populated even while we are sleeping. And suppose the fantasy of space (or time) travel were achieved in the near or far future: wouldn't we still, and inevitably, take our minds with us on the voyage? I remember again the re-locatory journey with which I began this essay: 'The experience was planetary,' I wrote, and indeed it was. But the planet above which I flew on my way back to Sydney: was that the earth itself, that we live upon? Or was it the earth in my mind? Or a dream earth, neither one nor the other but somehow both? A sane answer would have to conclude that it was all of these. In the same way, this fine collection of essays explores, in an idiosyncratic, generous and intelligent manner, the real- or virtual-world places where their authors go, the mind and the archival traces with which they orient their travel and the subsequent record—surely a palimpsest—they make of their journeys.

By way of a conclusion, here is the Portuguese writer, Fernando Pessoa, in the guise of his semi-heteronym, Bernardo Soares, riffing on a sentence of Thomas Carlyle's from his 1836 book, *Sartor Resartus*. '"Any road," said Carlyle, "even this road to Entepfuhl, will take you to the end of the world." But the Entepfuhl road, if taken in its entirety, and to the end, goes back to Entepfuhl; so Entepfuhl, where we already are, is that very end of the world we were seeking.' This is no doubt correct; but it is salutary to remind ourselves that these words were written in Lisbon, the capital of the first European world empire and the repository, some say, of traces of all the cities that have ever been or ever will be. All places may be found there; all times too. Africa, America, India, China, the Antipodes and the East.

This, for me, absurdly, is true also of Ohakune, which is a type of Entepfuhl; Entepfuhl means duck pond. Ohakune, we used to say, is a dump; but a dump is a kind of archive and from an archive you can find a way to elaborate memories and dreams as well as stories. Everything is there, including the absences. In the end, in whatever duck pond we might call home, in whichever place we say we come from, it is through the engagement of a questing mind with the many and various, actual and virtual, dimensions of what I'm calling PlaceTime that meaning is made. Any road will take you to the end of the world; if you get far enough away, as the song has it, you'll be on your way back home.

Notes on Sources:

The story 'The Garden of Forking Paths' appears in *Labyrinths*, by Jorge Luis Borges, ed. Donald E. Yates and James E. Irby (New York, New Directions, 1962).
The passage about Entepfuhl appears in *The Book of Disquiet*, by Fernando Pessoa, ed. Maria José de Lancastre, trans. Margaret Jull Costa (London: Serpent's Tail, 1991), 7

Martin Edmond was born in Ohakune and grew up there and in other small New Zealand towns. Since 1981, he has lived in Sydney. Edmond has written ten nonfiction books, and a number of shorter volumes of essays or other prose excursions, as well as half a dozen films. In 2013 he received the Prime Minister's Award for Literary Achievement for Nonfiction. Also in 2013, Edmond completed a Doctorate of Creative Arts at Western Sydney University. His dissertation, a biographical study of the two watercolour painters, was published as *Battarbee and Namatjira* by Giramondo in 2014. He holds the 2015 Creative New Zealand Michael King Writer's Fellowship and is working on a study of four distinguished expatriate New Zealanders. His most recent book is a memoir, *The Dreaming Land* (2015).